BECOMING YOU

ALSO BY TAMARACK SONG

Truthspeaking
Ancestral Ways to Hear and Speak the Voice of the Heart

The Talking Circle
A Traditional Decision-Making and Conflict Resolution
Process for All People and Occasions

Wilderness Stress and Trauma Management
For All Outdoor Programs, Guides, and Explorers

The Wilderness Stress and Trauma Management Workbook
A Quick-Reference and Training Guide

Journey to the Ancestral Self
Remembering What It Is to Be Human

Blossoming the Child
A Guide to Primal Parenting

The Healing Nature Trail
Forest Bathing for Recovery and Awakening

A Forest Bathing Companion
The Rejuvenating Power of a Healing Nature Trail Walk

Zen Rising
366 Sage Stories to Enkindle Your Days

Song of Trusting the Heart
A Classic Zen Poem for Daily Meditation

Whispers of the Ancients
Native Tales for Teaching and Healing in Our Time (with Moses Amik Beaver)

Fat Moons and Hunger Moons
The Turn of the Seasons for Northwoods Natives (with Moses Amik Beaver)

Like a Shadow
The Life and Training of a Guardian Warrior

Becoming Nature
Learning the Language of Wild Animals and Plants

Entering the Mind of the Tracker
Native Practices for Developing Intuitive Consciousness
and Discovering Hidden Nature

Extreme Survival Meat
A Guide for Safe Scavenging, Pemmican Making, and Roadkill

See www.snowwolfpublishing.org for an updated
list of Tamarack's publications.

BECOMING YOU

3 STEPS TO EMOTIONAL FREEDOM
AND WHAT KEEPS YOU FROM IT

TAMARACK SONG

SNOW WOLF PUBLISHING

7124 Military Road, Three Lakes, Wisconsin 54562

www.snowwolfpublishing.org

Snow Wolf Publishing is a division of Teaching Drum Outdoor School.

Copyright © 2023 by Tamarack Song

Song, Tamarack, 1948—

Becoming You: 3 Steps to Emotional Freedom and What keeps You From It.

ISBN: 9780996656153

Cover, text design, and layout by JamesBookDesigns.Weebly.com

Cover artwork by an anonymous contributor.

To send correspondence to the author of this book, mail a first-class letter to the author c/o Snow Wolf Publishing, 7124 Military Road, Three Lakes, Wisconsin 54562; or email the author at office@snowwolfpublishing.org.

Visit the author's websites at www.healingnaturecenter.org, www.teachingdrum.org, www.snowwolfpublishing.org, and www.brotherwolffoundation.org.

To Dream Again

When I was a kid, I'd splash in puddles
and throw rotten tomatoes at the shed
for the sheer joy of watching them explode

Where has it gone, that passion of youth?
What has bled the joy from dreams?
Have they bent to fears and beliefs?
To blame that brings shame?
To therapists as best friends?

Come sit with me
and we'll heal our fear
so we can play in puddles
and pelt tomatoes at old notions
that keep us pained and lonely

Part I

The 3 Steps to Emotional Freedom

Like Grandmother's Singing Bones

The Pima-Papago Indians of the Southwestern United States tell the story of an old woman who lived with her two grandchildren near a high, steep mountain. One day she told the children that a plant their people eat grows on the mountain, and she had made up her mind to go and gather some for her family.

When she got to the foot of the mountain, she could not see the top. Yet she was determined to climb it. With her cane in one hand and her power song riding her breath, she began to clamber up.

She grew weary as morning wore on and turned into afternoon. Sitting down to rest, she looked ahead, and still the top did not seem any nearer than when she started at dawn. Still, she got up and kept climbing, singing as she went.

Having to stop and rest many times throughout the afternoon, she didn't reach the summit meadow where the plant grew until evening. She suffered all the way: Her feet were blistered and bloody from the jagged rocks, and her legs were terribly scratched up from thorns.

At last she stood before the plant! With renewed energy, she tugged and tugged to pull it out of the ground. Only she pulled too hard, and as the plant let loose, she tumbled backward. Not able to catch herself, she rolled down the mountainside with plant in hand.

Boulders that she loosened bowled over her, and she bounced back and forth between everything that stood in her path. When she reached the base of the mountain, all that was left of her lifeless body was shredded flesh and a jumble of bones.

Yet after a short while, her bones picked themselves up, grabbed the plant, and started toward home singing her power song.[1]

Healing is a process of death and rebirth. It does not leave us the same person, but rather more like our true selves. Those accustomed to our wounded selves may not recognize us. It does not matter how old, tired, or disillusioned we are when we begin our healing journey. What does matter is that we begin, remaining present every step of the way.

Weariness, thorns, and stones are waiting for us. Rather than fight them, we embrace them as part of the *Path*, and we learn to move with them. The grandmother was not the first to walk the Path to the summit. And we are here to make sure she is not the last. Like hers, our journey is personal, though it is not done in isolation. We heal ourselves so that we may better engage in healthy relationships with others, to better sing the song of who we are in the *Web of Life* that surrounds us.

How We Heal

The method for healing ourselves involves three steps:

1. **Give what we want to receive.** We must be open before we can be filled. When we live from a perspective of relationship and support others in their healing, we also begin to heal.

2. **Feed what we want to grow.** Energy and enrichment follow attention. When we focus on what we want to grow, instead of the opposite, we nourish our vision and give it form.

3. **Surround ourselves with what we want to become.** When we change our surroundings, we alter ourselves. When we stay

CONTENTS

Dedication

After decades of often-grinding personal healing work, I didn't have the remotest desire to write a book on the topic. Only after my esteemed editor Leah Moss and I started to work together on our healing did I realize that our shared experience could be a metaphor for others' healing journeys.

I present *Becoming You* in Leah's honor, as she is to a large degree responsible for its content and quality. Since the beginning of our relationship, she has been one of my strongest inspirations and most helpful critics. My fondest hope is that the spirit she brings to this book empowers you on your way to wellness.

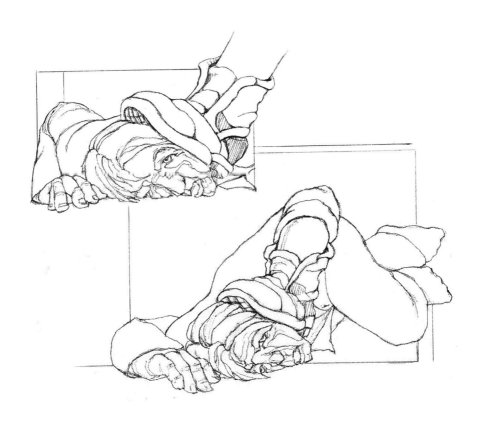

Prologue: My Story

"Where is this person coming from?" is the question I typically ask when I crack open a new book. My answer for you is: from experiences of desperation. This book is largely autobiographical. Though you will find material from my doctoral work in trauma recovery and suicide prevention, along with wisdom from indigenous elders I studied with, most of what I share on these pages is learned from direct experience.

Being the eldest child, I inherited from my absent, alcoholic father the responsibility of caring for my frantic mother. Early on, I learned the warning signs of emotional overload, depression, and suicide. As a young adult, I drifted in and out of numerous dysfunctional relationships. My college buddy, the friend who helped establish my wilderness skills school, and two of my former students, committed suicide. I still don't fully understand what stopped me a fraction of an inch from plunging a butcher knife into my chest one stormy day in the throes of my turbulent post-adolescence.

Family Legacy

Out of desperation grew my lifelong affair with addiction. I've found the most accessible doorway to the addictive aspects of my personality to be the legacy of my immediate family. Throughout my childhood, my father was a stoic, emotionally distant figure. Priding himself in his perfectionism and logical approach to life, he demanded the same of his offspring. Only he often failed to meet his own expectations, which he internalized from his relationship with his dominating twin brother. Add to that the ideation inspired by the mushrooming post-World War II material culture.

Dad found solace and socialization in his almost daily after-work tavern stops. We three sons learned well by example, and for a year or so all four of us were simultaneously active alcoholics. At age 20, after being placed on social probation in college for disruptive behavior while inebriated, I did a complete about-face and became a teetotaler. My focus turned to pacifism and Vietnam War draft resistance.

For the next thirty years, I didn't touch a drop of alcohol. In recent years, I've become at least a nominal social animal, and I now enjoy an occasional glass of quality beer or wine when out with friends.

My father and brothers did not fare as well with their addictive tendencies. Dad committed what I call *walking suicide,* which is conducting one's life with seeming disregard for health and well-being. At age 52, when he died of an apparent heart attack, he looked like he was 72.

His youngest son, four years my junior, bragged for decades about not drinking a drop of water. He kept hydrated on beer. But no more—the county elder protection agency recently placed him against his will in a care facility. In their estimation, he was no longer able to adequately care for himself due to advancing alcohol-induced dementia.

The middle son, who is three years my junior, lost job after job after college due to constant and excessive alcohol consumption. When he was about 25 years of age, I conducted a personal intervention, resulting in him committing himself to an alcoholism treatment facility. Many people called the effort a success, as he did suspend his dependence on alcohol. However, he retained his dependency by becoming a Jehovah's Witness. Now, forty years later, he is an elder in his local congregation.

Behavioral Adaptations

For each of the four of us, our addictive patterns took different forms. On one extreme was my youngest brother, who nearly always drank alone. On the other end, I drank only in a social context. My dad and middle brother imbibed both socially and alone. These tendencies point to the various behavioral and relational patterns we each adopted in order to survive.

My mother coped with my dad's emotional distance and cruelty by becoming a frantic and dutiful housewife. She gave her all to providing for us children and compensating for our largely absent father. That left her with little energy for her children's emotional nurturance. Bouts of crying and screaming became her stress release mechanisms.

Mom was my role model for how to survive emotional abuse and negligence. At the same time, I was given the challenge to endure a home environment that was bankrupt in nurturance and flush with trauma flashbacks—all awash in an unrelenting state of anxiety. My survival strategies fell into three categories:

1. Addictive Tendencies

I needed something to turn to in my life that was readily available, unchangeable, and reliable in its effect. As a young boy, I turned to artwork and Nature. In my adolescent years, it was sex and Nature. Then, as a young adult, I immersed myself in social change and Nature. (By the way, please note that I am here referring to *addictive tendencies* rather than *addictive substances*. I will explain why later.)

2. Enabling Patterns

In my parents' home, I only felt momentarily victimized. On the surface it appeared that I was overpowered and manipulated, but I had three things in my favor: Nature, my fantasies, and my intelligence. The diorama of my life was such that I wanted to escape by going to live with my cousins. That being impossible, I learned how to survive by developing enabling skills.

I learned how to appease my father so that he would not take his frustrations out on my mother. I learned how to sneak around my mother so that I could get my needs met without triggering a frantic emotional response from her. I covered for my father in my neighborhood playgroup whenever talk came up about why he was still in bed at noon or why he came home late every evening.

Carrying these enabling patterns into my adult life, I used them whenever there was emotional turmoil. I needed a peaceful environment in order to maintain centeredness and functionality, and I arranged for it with the skillset I best knew.

3. Escape Mechanisms

Along with running toward Nature and down numerous age-specific avenues, I had a built-in escape mechanism—Attention Deficit Disorder (ADD). In my tiny elementary school, there were four grades in each of the two rooms. I felt stupid and shamed when in first and second grade the nun would call on me for an answer and I didn't have it. However, if she would have quizzed me on what the third and fourth graders were learning, she might have advanced me a grade or two. I used nearly anything that lay to the right or left of what I was supposed to be doing as an escape.

I was wired for panoramic attention, which allowed me to escape the emotional intensity of the moment, in order to maintain my psycho-emotional well-being. It didn't matter whether the situation was potentially engendering or defaming. I simply had no reserve for either experiencing or processing it, due to my ever-draining and debilitating state of anxiety.

A note on my brothers' enabling patterns, addictive tendencies, and escape mechanisms: My youngest brother resorted to detachment and anger, which sometimes took the form of belligerence. Our middle brother seemed to be sandwiched between the two of us for protection. He took the quiet, easy-going route. Seldom speaking up, he never took sides, and he worked hard to get straight As in school. In each of us boys, there were morphed versions of our parents. We manifested the same adaptive patterns and coping mechanisms as they did, only often in different guises.

Craving Misery

Enabling and addictive tendencies feed *codependency* (defined as reliance on another person for approval and identity, which in turn supports that person's dysfunctions). My parents appeared to torment each other as they wallowed in the misery of the cultural and family legacies they manifested.

The two of them fit together like butter on bread. They relied on each other in numberless ways, and they pined for each other when they were apart. There is the saying that *Misery loves company*, but it was more than that. It's the same reason a severely abused spouse decides to go back to the relationship after she has been given a clear path to liberation and assurances of safety. It's the same reason a child acts out even though it leads to punishment. They (and so many others) have found it to be the only way to get some semblance of caring.

My early friendships and intimate relationships were of such a codependent nature. I learned to disguise those relationships under the veil of normalcy, yet they were intrinsically codependent. Even with all the inner healing work I've done, my tendency toward codependency in relationships persists.

As I finish my story, I'm left wondering how much I turn to escape mechanisms to find a supportive cultural context—and to ease the trauma burden I carry. And how many others with trauma-derived addictive personalities are doing the same? That may be fodder for another sharing. Right now, I have accomplished my goal of introducing you to where I am coming from on this journey to emotional freedom, and I invite you to continue on with me.

Imagine

... a healing approach that is seamlessly integrated into daily life.
... self-care techniques with successful track records that span millennia.

... a self-sustaining mode of healing that, once put in place, works by itself.

Imagine we must. We live in a society that doesn't require the best of us—a society that goes one further and calls us *sick*. And we accept that label. Being creatures of habit and pattern, we have a natural tendency to keep repeating what is familiar to us—even if it is self-destructive. We cope by keeping track of our neuroses and finding purpose in our pain. In essence, we take for granted our own insanity.

Our idea of mental illness is largely a myth. The real illness is embedded in our culture and belief systems. Forty years of living in the wilderness, living with Wolves, communing with *Native Elders**, studying world cultures, working as a counselor—and above all, living with myself—have taught me another way. It's one that understands our natural capacity and heals emotional wounds in a manner that is integrative and immediate. I don't think a single one of us would torture our feet with any old pair of shoes we came across, yet we do as much with our psyches when we settle for a healing method that is not custom fit.

Healing Organically

If we fulfill our basic obligations and remain reasonably functional, we can coast along forever being emotionally crippled. We seem to be incapable of understanding our sickness or doing anything about it without professional help and a long-term commitment. Not so with our hunter-gatherer ancestors. If they were not fully present in the now, if they were not fully engaged emotionally and physically, they were simply eliminated from the gene pool.

Every day was one of engagement, functioning with others as a cohesive whole, communicating clearly and directly, acting with

---

* Glossary terms are italicized the first time they appear in the text.

respect and empathy, honoring Elders and children; without that, the clan would either fall apart or be imperiled. Their healing was continual, spontaneous, and intrinsic to everyday life. By nature, their social environment was a healing environment.

This is the way we evolved—our genetic heritage. We are fully capable of being centered, present, and joyful; it is imprinted in our DNA, and our being continually strives to restore that state. Our self-healing is innate.

The reason healing organically (the method offered in this book) works is that we are still hunter-gatherers. Although we no longer live as hunter-gatherers, our genetic makeup has not changed significantly since we left the forest for the concrete jungle. This book, then, offers no new healing theories or modalities. Instead, it gets right down to what works now and has worked for millennia.

And I didn't have to go far to rediscover it. At the core of nearly all the contemporary healing approaches I have studied, I found three traditional principles that our ancestors used in their everyday lives:

1. **Give** what you want to receive.
2. **Feed** what you want to grow.
3. **Surround** yourself with what you want to become.

Going Right to the Core

In their clear, undiluted form, the three principles I just listed are the most organic way to heal and maintain wellness. They directly address our core wound: the old and deeply embedded family and cultural trauma. It has an insidious way of remaining hidden, as it takes on many guises when it surfaces, usually in the form of addictive behaviors and dysfunctional relationship patterns. When we do not know the source of these issues, we end up focusing on them as if they were the source. In effect, we address the symptoms rather than the cause.

This only perpetuates the problem. The Tlingit tribe of the American northwest tells the story of a vicious man-eating giant confronted by one of their esteemed warriors. He attacks and fatally wounds the giant, who with his last breath vows to keep forever preying upon all the world's humans. In an effort to prevent that, the warrior incinerates the giant's body and scatters the ashes to the wind. The dark cloud transforms immediately into a swarm of mosquitos. Along with the first sting of the mosquitoes, the man hears a booming voice: "I swear to you, I will feast upon you people until the end of time!"

The paradox is that the root of the giant's malice—his core wound—goes unknown and unaddressed, which is why he is continually reborn as a menace to life.

Healing from Within

There is a certain familiarity with issues stemming from our core wound. Whether we fully recall it or not, there was a dreadful event or period in our life that caused our essential self to retreat into a deep inner void where that self could feel safe. From then on, our ego took over, creating and projecting an image of self that would serve as a stand-in while protecting who we really are: the person we tucked safely away. We live with the sense that there is something more to who we are: something big, something that would make our lives different if we were connected to it. Without it, we go through our days as though we are lost, disconnected from ourselves. In fact, many of us are.

Our healing begins in an unorthodox way: Instead of searching *for* our center, we come *from* our center. A structure can only be as stable as the foundation upon which it is built—imagine what a difference it could make if we were centered and trusting when we *began* our behavioral rebuilding rather than starting with the fear and defensiveness of an entrenched ego.

We are starting from the inside, from a place of intrinsic trust and self-knowing. It is the place where the most true-to-self communication occurs: beyond words, in the realm of intuition and feeling. It is the rich fruit of ourselves that we have forgotten. It is there that the deep healing occurs.

We cannot ignore the core wound, nor can we revel in it. Instead, we go beyond the pain, to the core of who we are—which is and always has been whole, healed, and radiant. Rather than starting wounded and beat down, we right away reconnect with this core self. Losing touch with our true self is, after all, the very reason we became emotionally disabled in the first place.

Think of it as reinhabiting ourselves. There is nothing new about this approach where the heart connection comes first and the words come last. It is as old as the time of the first shamans and the first vision quest on a sacred mountain. It goes back to when our earliest ancestors stared into the embers of their hearthfires. There were few words and there was no drawn-out process—there was only the now, a person, and her soul.

It is like being inside a warm house and looking out into the cutting cold rather than being out there and shivering uncontrollably as we look plaintively through the window at the cozy fireplace. Imagine what a difference that change in perspective could make in our healing journey.

The Way Home

This book lays bare the essence of the healing process, so we may begin to heal ourselves in the most essential ways. In Part I we explore the three traditional principles for becoming and being well. The final step, surrounding ourselves with what we want to become, may be the hardest and most important. After all, if we put our fresh apple back in a dirty fridge with other rotten apples, it is virtually guaranteed to rot.

In Part II we examine the twelve ways we keep feeding our pain. Behind nearly every failed attempt at healing, behind nearly every person who is chronically depressed or whose life and relationships are continually dysfunctional, several of these twelve practices are active.

Once we admit these naked truths, we are ready to start leaving behind our legacy of self-hate, depression, and failed relationships. I don't mean after two or ten years; we can heal as fast as we can throw that moldy, mushy thing in the compost, clean out the fridge, then grab a bright, fresh one to bite into.

We live in a blame-shame culture, where we hold others responsible for our condition then expect others to fix it. The problem lies not with the counselors or authors whom we turn to, as what they have to offer can prove valuable later on in our process. The issue is that we turn to outside guidance first. Institutions and practitioners have taken over our self-care, while we have lost our ability to care for ourselves.

The healing we need is based on personal responsibility and a desire for deep change *now*. It is not for the faint of heart. It is not for those seeking a guru. It is for those who sense that a new life lies before them—for those who realize it begins within them.

There is no need to trust that this book is going to work for you; there is no waiting period that requires faith—you are feeling and doing better *right away*. What's more, the only person this book asks you to trust is *yourself*—your true self, a wise being who knows just what you need. In fact, your true self is the *only* person who knows just what you need.

Some people, as they begin to heal, become self-conscious about being labeled *sick*. When I have a virus, I have a sickness—I feel and look sick. However, this does not mean I am a sick person. When I have a broken bone that needs to heal, it doesn't mean there is something intrinsically wrong with my body. The same is true of my psycho-emotional state: I am fundamentally whole and balanced, regardless of my behavioral patterns. What needs healing are the wounds I began incurring at a very early age from running the gauntlet of life in my family and culture.

Healing is a necessary part of life that occurs continually in each and every one of us throughout our bodies and psyches. Healing is not only natural, it is also necessary, so let's embrace and support it. Considering our entrenched cultural narratives about healing, this new approach may be just a glimmer in your imagination. A flicker of possibility. Yet as we progress through this book, its contours take form, blossoming into a new reality—your reality.

Chapter in a Page

Our idea of mental illness is largely a myth. The real illness stems from a culture that labels us sick and dependent. The opposite is true: We have a natural capacity to heal our emotional wounds in a way that is integrative and immediate.

In our society, we ta ble our *sickness* with professional help that entails a long-term commitm. t. Provided we fulfill our basic obligations, we can coast along forever being emotionally crippled. Yet for our hunter-gatherer ancestors, healing was continual, spontaneous, and intrinsic to everyday life. Survival required being fully present, emotionally and physically. Instead of endless once-a-week appointments, our ancestors worked daily with others, communicating clearly, directly, and respectfully to keep the clan from falling apart.

This is how we evolved—it is our genetic heritage. We are fully capable of being centered, present, and joyful: It is imprinted in our DNA, so our being continually strives to restore that state.

At the core of most contemporary healing approaches, I found three traditional principles used by our ancestors:

1. **Give** what you want to receive.
2. **Feed** what you want to grow.
3. **Surround** yourself with what you want to become.

First, instead of searching *for* our center, we come *from* our center.
We start from that place of intrinsic trust and self-knowing—per-
petually whole, healed, and radiant. After all, sickness is not our
essence. My broken bone doesn't mean something is intrinsically
wrong with my body. The same is true of my psycho-emotional state.

This healing approach requires personal responsibility and a desire
for deep change *now*. This book asks you to trust yourself—the true
self who knows just what you need. A new life is possible and begins
within. Healing is natural and necessary, so let's embrace and support it.

Please note: This book is not a cure-all—no book will do that
for you. Although the approach presented here can transform
the issues you struggle with in your everyday life, there is no
substitute for the deep somatic work on the trauma memories
that lie at the root of those issues. To address the childhood,
cultural, and epigenetic (ancestral) traumas that nearly all of us
carry, please see my book *Breaking the Trauma Code*.

put, we remain stuck. To heal ourselves we must be immersed in a healing environment.

Each step can stand alone or be applied as part of a sequence, though when combined, the three steps work synergistically, enabling us to change more quickly and thoroughly. Prepare to find that each step complements the others; when working in sync, they may even be indistinguishable from one another. As we begin to apply them to daily life, we do so with patience, lest—like the grandmother—we stumble when our goal is at hand.

First, Give What We Want to Receive

In a real sense, there is no self-healing—it is relational and premised on giving. Our identities are formed in a web of relationship, which extends beyond our skin and encompasses all the people in our lives. Our very existence is predicated upon this web. Our healing, then, is embedded in the web. It asks that we act from a place of Circle Consciousness, where giving is receiving and receiving is giving. It is a mindset and a way of life that we cannot access alone.

When we live for ourself, we end up with just that: ourself. When we live for and with the Life around us, we become filled with Life. Later we discuss how being in pain means we are actually in a position to become healed. This concept can be expanded upon to create the scaffolding for living a life that is whole and healed:

- **Be open,** in order to be filled.
- **Trust,** in order to be trusted.
- **Be vulnerable,** in order to be cherished.
- **Be humble,** so that we can be self-empowered.
- **Be self-critical,** so that we can be self-accepting.

This can be summarized simply in one statement: *Giving is receiving*—and we need to give before we can receive.

We are social creatures, so our natural tendency is to be helpful, share what we have, and aid those in need. Ohiyesa, a Santee Dakota from the 1800s, says of the *Native*: "He is always ready ... to impoverish himself to please his friend."[2] A Native person often gifts anonymously; he customarily strives to give without expectation of anything in return. By living in a trusting environment, where the feeling of relationship extends to all of life, the Native learns that when she is giving, she has already received. She knows from experience that when she gives of herself, for the pure bliss of sharing, she keeps the doorway open to all the gifting that is intended for her.

My Elders call this the *Gifting Way*: the state of abundance and personal fulfillment that comes, often seemingly without effort, from living the natural law that giving is receiving. This is what it means to walk the Path of Life with others and to live in Circle Consciousness. In healing parlance, this translates to: When I can support someone else in his or her healing, I progress in my own healing. Or put simply, *When you heal, I heal.*

Nature's Way

Imagine you are an organ within a functioning organism, let's say the liver in a human body. You take care of the waste and store energy for the heart, lungs, muscles, and all the other bodily components. In turn, they provide you with nutrients, oxygen, mobility, and so on. You and the other organs are involved in one continual exchange, where giving and receiving cannot be distinguished one from the other.

In our culture, we have been taught to see giving and receiving in the matrix of cause and effect: We give because we received, and we receive because we gave. From a Native perspective, this is simplistic and one-dimensional. We give and receive since we are Mother Earth's children, thus we are the beneficiaries of her caring. Being one with the eternal flow of energy that runs through and around us, we have no choice except to give, nor do we have a choice with receiving. Whether or not we are mindfully involved in the process, we are still giving and receiving. Every unconscious exhalation of ours nourishes the vegetation around us with carbon dioxide, while every unconscious inhalation is the vegetation nourishing us.

Imagine a web of infinite, interconnected strands that come and go in countless directions, creating myriad forms and shapes. The relationship among the strands, forms, and shapes is symbiotic and without limitation. This results in unbounded mutual support rather than a cyclical, karmic, or polar relationship with clear boundaries and directions. Who gives to whom and who receives from whom is a moot point, since all are simultaneously giving and receiving to the whole, which is giving and receiving to itself.

A maple forest is a favorite example of mine. Maple trees drop their leaves without withdrawing the nutrients from them. The leaves collect on the forest floor, creating a rich mulch that supports a host of life, from mushrooms and wildflowers to succulent herbs and berry bushes. Insects, salamanders, birds, and deer are supported by the plants. When these plants and animals die and decompose, the nutrients are taken up by the Maples, who end up all the richer for their giving. Our healing operates in the same way: When we forget about ourselves and give to someone else for the pure sake of giving, we are not forgotten. Again, when you heal, I heal.

Gifting with No Strings Attached

A wealthy matron donated a large sum of money to a monastery to build a needed addition. When she took it to the monastery abbot, he replied, "Yes, I will receive it."

Confused by the abbot's response, the matron said, "There is a large sum of money in that bag that I just gave you."

"Are you waiting for me to thank you for it?" asked the abbot.

The matron replied, "Is it not what is typically done?"

"I believe it is the giver who should be thankful," stated the abbot.

There is a Greenland Eskimo saying: *Gifts make slaves like whips make dogs.* Our culture sees giving and receiving as highly trans-actional—we give with the expectation of receiving something in return, even if it is only an acknowledgment of the exchange or a sign of gratitude. In most traditional cultures, and in nature's way, this expectation is absent. The Maples simply drop their leaves.

Giving and receiving as we know it is based upon our concept of surplus and want: a reality we constructed when we became agriculturalists, dependent upon boom-and-bust crop cycles. This made it impossible for us to remain functioning in the gifting economy, where *gift* is defined as something given purely for the giving.

A Native has no use for surplus; it bogs her down. She is nearly always surrounded by abundance. The wealth she has use for—the treasure that makes sense in her life—is that of character and vision. Material wealth gets in the way of that. She follows the example of the Wolf, who leaves the part of his kill he does not need so that Raven and Fox and Chickadee may feast upon it. Neither Native, Wolf, nor Chickadee need to be concerned with herding or cultivating, as their Earth Mother does it for them. Here is giving and receiving in its purest, least dichotomized form.

Some Native Peoples hold what are called *Giveaways* or *Potlatches*, which are ceremonial events during which individuals who have accumulated surplus distribute it to those more in need. Ohiyesa, the Santee Dakota from the late 1800s, says: "Public giving is a part of every important ceremony. It properly belongs to the celebration of birth, marriage, and death and is observed whenever it is desired to do special honor to any person or event. Upon such occasions, it is common to literally give away all that one has to relatives, to guests of another tribe or clan, but above all to the poor and the aged, from whom we can hope for no return."[3]

Possessiveness and hoarding may seem to favor the individual, yet in the natural realm, the well-being of the individual is dependent upon the well-being of the group. This requires that we give before we receive. A flock of Chickadees survives predation from Hawks when each individual within the flock is strong, as well as when each cooperates with the others for food, shelter, and protection. The smaller the group, the more vulnerable it becomes. It is the natural way of relationship and Circle Consciousness: When you are safe, I am safe; when you are well, I am well; when you are healed, I am healed.

The Impossibility of Self-Love

Giving and receiving in our culture is often bound up in the concept of love—perhaps the greatest thing that we can either give or receive. Many of us are allured by the idea that *self-love* is key to living whole and healed lives, and that the relationship that matters most is the one we have with ourselves. While it may be true that a healthy relationship with one's self is important to healing, self-love is inextricably bound to love of others.

Anthropologist Colin Turnbull tells us that "love, however defined, implies duality of some kind ... it cannot feed on itself."[4] Another way of expressing this is that *love is relationship*, and this is the definition I am using in this discussion.

Is self-love even possible? We can provide for ourselves, and we can be kind to ourselves. However, to love another is the only way to be loved. Here again, we must be willing to give more before we receive. The reason is that if we first ask for love, we are probably doing so to not appear vulnerable. We are acting from a defensive position, which in effect constructs boundaries that inhibit us from giving love.

In Nature, we see Wolves, Dolphins, and various birds bringing gifts to create trust and an opening for reciprocal love. They give first, so that they can receive. We do the same by bringing gifts when we are courting.

Yet when we are emotionally or physically wounded, the ego steps in and takes a defensive position. We are hurt and don't want to be further injured, so as a protective mechanism we withhold our love or withdraw it from others. We become incapable of unconditional love. This limits the potential of a relationship, as we are able to receive only what we are able to give. *Self-love, then, is actually the love that we allow in from others.*

Healing Touch

An effective way to dissolve boundaries to love is through caring touch. When we are touched by others, we sidestep our ego and the defenses it has emplaced. Our pituitary gland is stimulated to release oxytocin, a hormone that supports human bonding. We experience an increase in trust and a decrease in fear and anxiety. It is known as the *tribal hormone*, as it encourages social behavior and group empathy.

Notice I said "When we are touched *by others* ..." rather than just saying "When we are touched." According to Dr. Arthur Janov, psychologist and creator of *Primal Therapy*, "If you rub an animal's belly, oxytocin levels rise. If you lick her, oxytocin also rises, but if you rub yourself it won't. You cannot love yourself."[5]

HOLISTIC HEALING

You may have heard of *hands-on healing*, or *healing touch*, which practitioners and beneficiaries claim has physical healing powers. Recent research shows that, along with affecting psycho-emotional healing, oxytocin reduces inflammation and encourages fast wound healing.[6] Stress, on the other hand, significantly slows wound healing.[7]

The major impediment to receiving healing touch is probably a love-deprived childhood. In the words of Dr. Janov, "Once you are unloved throughout your childhood, it is imprinted—you are unloved and feel unloved even when you don't know it. It drives all later behavior."[8] For many of these people, healing touch is initially ineffective.

Here is a five-step process for creating a healing touch environment capable of surmounting childhood conditioning. The points are listed in descending order of importance, which is crucial here since each preceding point is essential to implementing the next point.

Opening the Portal to Healing Touch

1. **Choose a location** that feels safe to you and will remain interruption-free.

2. **Select a trusted friend** or practitioner.

3. **Set a time limit** in advance that is mutually agreed upon.

4. **Proceed slowly,** with whatever form of physical touch feels mutually comfortable.

5. **Speak up** whenever you feel uncomfortable proceeding, for any reason.

If you reacted either neutrally or positively to the session, relax into wordlessness immediately after, for a period of time no less than a half-hour. This imprints the experience in your long-term memory. Then set a date for another session, and continue sessions at around three-day intervals until being touched by a trusted person elicits feelings of camaraderie rather than fear.

Some people ask me why I advocate a somatic approach such as healing touch rather than talk therapy. Others tell me that they have been working with their therapists for months, even years, with no discernible results. Here, in Dr. Janov's words, is my answer to them: "Cognitive therapy, focused in the present, which is what the left brain does, can help us understand the kind of situations or people to avoid but they cannot begin to touch the drive that makes it happen. They, and therefore the patient, never understands the unconscious. And never gets well. That includes the therapist who helps the patient skim along the top, never asking 'why?'" [9]

Leading with Honor and Respect

Our healing journeys are intensely personal, yet they are not solitary. To maximize our healing while getting to the truth of who we are, our healing must take place in the context of relationship. There may be times when all we want is to receive a cure; we feel as though we have nothing to give. In those moments, when I am unsure of what to give or how to give it, I turn to honor and respect. For me, to honor is to create space for listening, and respect is the actual listening. No matter where I am or whom I am with, I am always in a position to give these two things. And when I am able to give, I am able to receive and heal.

Chapter in a Page

Healing is not based on solitude—it is relational and premised on giving. Our web of relationship defines us and how we heal. We need to be open to others in order to be filled, to trust in order to be trusted, and to be vulnerable in order to be loved. Natives call this *the Gifting Way*: *Giving is receiving, and we must give before we can receive.* The Native knows when she gives for the pure bliss of sharing, she remains open to all the gifting intended for her. This is how we walk the Path of Life with others, revealing the truth in the saying *When you heal, I heal.*

Our culture sees giving and receiving as transactional: We give expecting something in return. In nature's way, giving and receiving flow continually with no sense of indebtedness.

Giving and receiving are key to love, which is perhaps the greatest thing we give or receive. Still, many think that self-love is central to a whole and healed life. While a healthy relationship with one's self may be important, loving another is the only way to be loved. Just as animals give of themselves when courting a mate, we need to give love to others—with no guarantee for reciprocation—before we can receive love.

Caring touch can dissolve boundaries to love. When we are touched by others, we sidestep our ego and its defenses. Our pituitary gland releases oxytocin, the *tribal hormone*, which supports human bonding. Oxytocin increases trust, decreases fear and anxiety, and encourages social behavior and group empathy. It also promotes the healing of physical wounds.

Finally, when we feel we have nothing to give, we can turn to honor and respect. I do this by creating space for listening (honor), then actually listening (respect). Whatever the circumstances, I can always give these two things. I am thus able to receive and heal.

Introduction to Part I / First, Give What We Want to Receive Endnotes

1 Richard Erdoes and Alfonso Ortiz, "The Transformed Grandmother," in *American Indian Myths and Legends* (Pantheon, 1984), 451-53.

2 Charles Alexander Eastman, *Indian Scout Talks* (Boston: Little, Brown, and Company, 1914), 190.

3 Charles Alexander Eastman, *The Soul of the Indian* (Houghton Mifflin, 1911), 100.

4 Colin M. Turnbull, *The Mountain People* (Simon & Schuster, New York), 237.

5 Dr. Arthur Janov, "On Loving Yourself," *Janov's Reflections on the Human Condition: The Simple Truth is Revolutionary*, last modified December 1, 2012, accessed 13 October 2020, http://cigognenews.blogspot.com/2012/12/on-loving-yourself.html.

6 Jean-Philippe Gouin, et al., "Marital Behavior, Oxytocin, Vasopressin, and Wound Healing," *Psychoneuroendocrinology* 35, no. 7 (2010): 1082-90.

7 Janice K. Kiecolt-Glaser, et al., "Slowing of Wound Healing by Psychological Stress," *The Lancet* 346, no. 8984 (1995): 1194-96.

8 Dr. Arthur Janov, "On Loving Yourself," http://cigognenews.blogspot.com/2012/12/on-loving-yourself.html.

9 Ibid.

Second, Feed What We Want to Grow

Giving and receiving is as much an exchange of energy as content. Energy follows attention; when we place our attention on something, our energy enriches it and makes it manifest. If we tend to a garden—watering its plants, nourishing its soil, and remaining attentive to its needs—then it grows; if we neglect the garden, it does not.

This method is the natural way of relationship: What we feed grows, and what we do not feed withers. Instead of expending energy trying to remove what we do *not* desire, we simply direct our attention to the things we *do* desire. This principle is the second phase in our shift from what keeps us stuck to what allows us to heal.

There is a finite amount of energy. If we use it to accentuate the positive, then naturally, what is out of balance has less power and must either shrink or change. There is a Maori proverb that says: *Turn your face to the sun, and the shadow will fall behind you.* We are creatures of habit and conditioning; when we take ownership of the direction of our energy, we can recondition ourselves to stand in the light instead of the shadows.

On the other hand, if we focus on the negative, it grows too. If we use our energy to *engage the enemy*, we manifest that figure, we give it power, then we become it. Yes, you heard it right: *We become the enemy.* When we live and act according to what we do not desire, we allow it to influence who and how we are. We feed our woundedness and starve our healing.

We create the psycho-emotional environments in which our bodies dwell. Just as stress and self-destructive thought patterns are causes of disease, so are comforting and supportive visualizations purveyors of health. Either we attempt to change others, and foster dissonance, or we can work on changing ourselves, and foster resonance. As you weigh these options, keep two things in mind:

1. **We cannot do both**—remember, there is a finite amount of energy.

2. **The healing journey is personal**—the only person we can change is ourself.

Empowerment Healing

Feeding what we want to grow makes healing engaging and empowering. First, we take responsibility for the situation. No matter what it is, who caused it, or who we think is to blame, this is the absolute first thing we must do, or we cannot be empowered. Waiting for someone else to apologize or assume responsibility is nothing more than enabling our dependence on another person. It might feel good in the short run when it assuages our fragile ego; however, in the long run it is self-destructive, as it robs us of our personal power and cripples our ability to move forward.

Second, we make peace with our flaws. A reliable sign of healthy people—those actively engaged in their healing process—is that they consciously express that they are good people even as they grow and learn from working through their dysfunctions. A reliable sign of people struggling with or resisting their healing is that they get down on themselves and others. They criticize, judge, and demonize. Those who are able to be honest and vulnerable about their healing journey are more likely to refrain from lashing out at themselves or others. They seek progress, not perfection.

There are going to be times when we struggle or regress. Those situations are not the end of our journey—they can become part of it, depending on how we respond to them. When we find ourselves stuck in a confrontational situation, or when we are reactive from being triggered by someone else's words or actions, here is the way to self-empowerment:

1. **Take unqualified responsibility** for the situation (not just what we consider to be our half, and not only if the other person does the same).

2. **Take a break** for 15 or 20 minutes, to let the adrenaline subside so we can separate fact from feeling.

3. **Process** what happened and what can be done about it, on both a feeling and a rational level.

The Healing Mentality

Empowerment healing is more about perception than anything else. In fact, nearly all healing, including physical healing, has a mental-emotional component that ought to be addressed.

Changing how we think is the basis of changing how we feel. At times, this mentality may seem like negligence, especially in our culture that elevates Western medical attention to paragon status. However, let me offer you the following story to consider:

Once one of the Guardian trainees at Teaching Drum Outdoor School had a finger infection spread to his hand—it was hot and swollen—and a red streak was working its way up his arm. Anybody in their right mind—or their rational mind, I should say— would ship him out at once for treatment, right? Here at Teaching Drum we respond from the limbic mind and emphasize the need to take personal responsibility for our healing.

What was happening to this Seeker involved much more than a clear-cut case of infection. It had to do with the mental-emotional perspective he lived by, which enabled the infection to spread. This Seeker had long been struggling with a passive approach to life in general; it reflected in the treatment of his wound, which he was not keeping up, even though he was adequately informed and repeatedly reminded. Addressing the infection alone would not get at this deeper problem.

When we came out to camp and saw the hand, we told him he was going in to the clinic right then and there if he didn't get a grip and immediately commence with the complete hot-cold-massage-shake treatment a minimum of six times per day. I knew it was possible for him to heal his affliction—the infection as well as the disengaged approach to life that was worsening his health by the day. The real problem was his psycho-emotional state.

If we had immediately taken him to get antibiotics, we would have treated the infection, yes, yet we also would have enabled him to continue living passively. He would have just ended up in another situation of helplessness and victimization, then another, and another ... The next time he injured himself, we would simply be repeating the cycle again by bringing him to the clinic.

Something happened when we told him the game was over: A dead-serious look washed over his face, and he realized he had to either shape up or take a trip to town, which he absolutely did not want to do. Right away he started to heat up a couple of rocks for the hot-cold part of the treatment. Instead of feeding what he did *not* want to grow, the infection, the Seeker fed what he desired: an engaged, active approach to life.

That still wasn't enough for me—since we were looking at this situation from the limbic mind and from the Native perspective, we saw this was a matter of Circle Consciousness. This Seeker's camp-mates were just as responsible for his condition as he was, as the organism is no stronger than the weakest organ. Once they were on board with him, I knew he was going to be okay. His healing involved more than just his mind and body—it affected everyone in his community, so all of us needed to take part as well.

Two days later when we walked into camp, he was beaming from ear to ear—he amazed even himself with how rapidly he turned the situation around. He could barely speak—he just held his nearly completely recovered hand up for us to see. It was an amazing sight, even though I've witnessed healings like this so many times over the years.

The point here is not to discredit conventional medicine. Rather, we wish to emphasize that our medical conditions have physical symptoms *and* psycho-emotional origins.

Responding to an Unhealthy Relationship

Healing, as you know from the previous chapter, is not accomplished in isolation. It's all about relationship. Sometimes we get caught in relationships that seem to work against our healing and growth. When we find ourselves in an unhealthy relationship and want to desist from it, we can do one of two things:

1. **We can blame the other person and attack him.** In this scenario, I typically externalize and blame and in one way or another, wreak havoc upon the other person. I consider this person the source of all my problems and use religion, history, friends, and anything else to support that belief. When I judge and attack this person, I am likely to receive the same treatment from him in return.

2. **We can take personal responsibility for our part in the relationship.** I am now an active participant in the relationship rather than a passive receptor and a victim. This perspective empowers me to assess my role in the relationship, take responsibility for it, and change/heal. I can give honor to my partner in the relationship, recognizing that he is also wounded and struggling from trying to survive in a sick culture. In this way, I honor him for his journey and leave the door open for growth and awareness and healing.

Only the second option supports our healing, as a relationship is nothing if it is not interactive and I have as much a part in creating the relationship as does the other person. Acknowledging our responsibility in a situation affirms our personal power. Without doing this, it becomes too easy to envision ourselves as helpless, hapless, and stuck in our lives. To be healed, we need to tap into our personal power—to do *that*, we first need to believe that power exists.

Fake It Until You Make It

If my heart is not in the healing process, I just fake it—that's right, fake it. Remember, humans are incredibly adept at deceiving others and ourselves (see *Part II, #10*), meaning we can, and may need, to make use of that skill to get us started. The most important thing is that we feed what we want to grow.

If I am an alcoholic and start acting sober, I am likely to become sober. If I am an enabler and keep acting like an enabler, I am likely to remain one. Every time I act out my pattern, I am reinforcing it, which makes it all the more difficult to change it. When I begin to act out a new pattern, however, I disrupt old neural connections and I begin to change how I live. When I direct my attention and my energy to this new pattern, it becomes my new reality.

It doesn't matter what I *think* or *feel* about the pattern; what I *do* is what I become. Thoughts and feelings come and go like the wind. It is my actions—and only my actions—that move me on my path. That define who I am. That leave a track. Sometimes my actions convince my mind and my heart rather than the other way around.

Once I start walking straight on my path, I gain the momentum to keep walking straight. It feels awkward at first, as I am used to bumbling, so all of my thoughts and feelings are based on that. In other words, my relationship to my walking is based on my past walking since that is all I have known. To develop a new relationship with my walking, I need to envision what my walking could be. To walk straight, I need to envision something to walk toward.

The most important thing, though, is that I begin to move. The power is in the walking, and those first steps take faith. The Hawai-ian Elder Kaili'ohe Kame'ekua of Kamalo, Moloka'i, who lived in the 1800s, said: "Small things are necessary before big things can be achieved."1 First steps may be small, yet their value is paramount.

For a while I may experience pain, as those first steps are contrary to everything I have grown accustomed to. I expect to get angry, frustrated, and self-critical. I may feel victimized and blame others. All of this stems from my feelings, which are carryovers from my past that do not fit my vision. Still, I keep walking. When my faith in my new path wanes, I simply look back and bear witness to how far I have already come. I grit my teeth and push forward.

Eventually, the awkwardness and feelings of alienation that come from doing something unfamiliar evaporate. In their place, I notice that I am feeling grounded and nourished—a new and welcome change! My vision grows stronger as it is gradually replaced by the new reality of the Now. I no longer need to go on faith. My tracks have grown strong and clear. All I have to do is look behind me to see the direction ahead.

Envisioning Ourselves

Imagine that as you are healing, you are also re-creating yourself, since from your ego's perspective, that is exactly what you are doing. You know who you are inside: your qualities, your abilities, your core self. You know how you would be if you were in prime physical shape, fully present, and sensitized to your surroundings. You know how you would feel about yourself and what relationships you would be capable of. Recognize that this person is already you. The vision is not unfounded—it doesn't come from nothing.

Now comes the leap of faith: You have to think it in order to make it. The reason is that your modus operandi—your habits and patterns, your reactive feelings, even the way you talk and move—are all learned behaviors based on who you aren't, who you created to take your place in order to protect yourself and survive. You need to trust in your re-created self, your real self, implicitly and explicitly, or you won't be able to let go of that puppet who has been holding your place.

Go ahead, try it out—speak the way that expresses the real you, move with the grace and sensitivity that reflects the fully conscious you, allow your face to relax and let the real you shine through. I know it doesn't feel right: It feels contrived, even pretentious. That's because our feeling self has evolved to reflect life as we know it, not as we would like it to be.

New feelings, new perceptions of myself, can grow and take the place of those old feelings that have been attached to my puppet self. I just need to realize that my actual self, my real self, has been locked away in a cold, sterile place and has had no opportunity to weave himself a warm blanket of complementary feelings. So you must have the sustaining faith to stand out alone in the cold, knowing that the feelings that give life its color are bound to come and that nourishing relationships and enriching experiences are ahead. It is more than a leap of faith—it is a belief in self.

As we confront this leap, we are overwhelmed by a sense of fear of what could be and also a great longing for it. As we are about to learn in *Part II, #7*, fear keeps us from satisfying our longing, and the inability to satisfy our longing keeps us in fear of being authentic in our relationships. Remember though, our fear is not an illness or something to be excised—it belongs with us and serves us as a guide on the Path of Life. Our duty is to embrace it, listen to it, and walk with it alongside us. We walk this Path moment by moment, one step at a time. As long as we feed what we want to grow, every step leads us closer to that vision of our true self: authentic, healed, and radiant.

Chapter in a Page

If we tend to a garden, it grows; neglect it, and it withers. This is the natural way of relationship. Instead of expending energy to remove what we do not desire, we focus on what we *do* desire.

There is a finite amount of energy. If we use it to accentuate the positive, what is out of balance has less power and must shrink or change. If we focus on what we do not desire, negativity can influence us. Recognize that we create the psycho-emotional environments our bodies dwell in. Just as stress and self-destructive thought patterns cause disease, comforting and supportive visualizations support health.

Empowerment healing involves two key directives. First, take unqualified responsibility for the situation. Waiting for someone else to apologize or assume responsibility enables our dependence on them. When we become an active participant in life, we engage our power to change and heal. Second, remember that we can be vulnerable and honest without victimizing ourselves. Focus on progress, not perfection.

Perception is the cornerstone of empowerment healing. Nearly all healing, even physical healing, has a mental-emotional component or origin. Personal responsibility means that we address our ailments and the lifestyle that created them.

Although perception is primary, actions are indispensable to the healing process. When we lose faith in ourselves or succumb to doubt, we can just fake it. Humans are incredibly adept at deception, so we might as well use that skill to get us started.

We pretend we are healing to give ourselves momentum; soon the momentum builds, and the healing becomes authentic. When I act out this new way of living, I disrupt old neural connections and begin to change. My attention and energy strengthen a new pattern, which becomes my new reality. This may be a leap of faith—more than that, it is a belief in my true self.

Second, Feed What We Want to Grow Endnotes

1   Koko Willis and Pali Jae Lee, *Tales from the Night Rainbow* (Night Rainbow Publishing, 1990), 30.

Third, Surround Ourselves with
What We Want to Become

"When we want to change, we surround ourselves with the people we most want to be like," a Blackfoot Elder told me years ago. Empowered healing involves first embracing our innate ability to take personal responsibility for the events in our lives, and to be self-reflective without self-victimizing. Then comes the transformative element: the Elderwisdom I just quoted, which is the focus of this chapter. It is enacted by directly immersing ourselves in what we want to become. The reasons for doing so are simple:

- When I change my surroundings, I change.
- When I stick with my surroundings, I stay stuck in my behavior.

According to Circle Consciousness, we are not just part of our Circle, we *are* our Circle. Healing is interactive, premised on relationships, and a reflection of the communities to which we belong. We become what we surround ourselves with, emotionally, culturally, environmentally. On the one hand, this can be dangerous, as we absorb the pain and woundedness that we surround ourselves with. On the other hand, we can use this principle to our advantage by surrounding ourselves with healing people—the people who through example and inspiration influence us to unfold into our intrinsic, balanced selves.

We find true, lasting healing in our Circle. The help of counselors can be invaluable at times; and at other times, it has its limitations. They can help bring awareness to our behavior, yet since they are not part of our everyday actions, they can only help with situations mainly in retrospect. The real healing work needs to occur on an everyday basis. Our real healing partners, then, are the people with whom we share our everyday lives and enact our patterned behaviors—the people who entrench the pattern or help us break it.

If we stay in the surroundings that formed our current state of being, it is further reinforced. Healthy and healing people encourage the same behaviors in me, and unfortunately, the reverse holds as well. So I consciously choose my company with the natural way—the healing way—in mind.

The same Elder also taught me that you can best tell who someone is by looking at the people with whom he or she associates. The reason is that life is not about us as individuals; it is about our relationships. Intertwined in a supportive web of relations, we begin to change with no more effort than being consciously present. And the change is fundamental since our environment is an immersion experience. We practice what we are learning within the context of our everyday life.

Immersion Healing Exercise

Below is an envisioning exercise that can help you break habits and patterns impeding your healing. The first column is for listing the habits you would like to break, the second column is for recording the environments in which you practice the habits (or the people associated with them), and the third column is for noting the changes in surroundings that you think might inspire and support your change in behavior. The examples are patterns and behaviors that I have healed myself from by using this method. For yourself, draw a chart like this one, and begin by listing what you would like to change about yourself. Then complete column two, and save the change column for last.

Old Habits and Patterns I Wanted to Break	Where Those Habits and Patterns Thrived	Changes That Supported New Habits and Patterns
Alcohol consumption	Bars, restaurants, and the company of alcohol consumers	Seeking solace, joy, and connection in non-alcoholic settings and with non-alcohol consumers
Marijuana smoking	The company of marijuana consumers and enthusiasts	Surrounding myself with people who neither consume nor advocate the consumption of marijuana
Inadequate exercise	Sedentary spaces or the company of idle people	Spending my time in active spaces and among active people who exercise
Workaholism	Fast-paced, urban settings and the company of workaholics	Seeking out slower-paced settings and the company of those who value rest
Casual intimacy	The company of serial romantics and people who engage in casual intimacy	Seeking connection with people who value sustained, long-term intimacy
Unwavering idealism	The company of unwavering idealists	Surrounding myself with those who are optimistic realists, self-reflective, and self-critical

Emotional Intelligence

What affects one of us affects us all. My joy and pain are yours and yours are mine. I consider it a privilege to help others in their healing, and even more than that, I see it as a necessity. Tibetan Buddhists call dwelling in this state of awareness *Bodhisattva* and consider it to be an advanced form of enlightenment. For me, it is merely acknowledgment that all things are related in the Hoop of Life, which is only common sense for a Native person.

In the Buddhist tradition, the first step to *Bodhisattva* is called *Bodhicitta,* or personal enlightenment (which is achieved by stepping beyond the ego, to be freed of the bounds of self). When an individual comes to realize that her seeking of enlightenment is not only for herself, but for everyone, and is willing to take on the pain of others in order to help them, then she has achieved a state of *Bodhisattva*.

According to my Elders, there is nothing exceptional about this state—it is the way of all natural life. From my Elders' perspective, it is exceptional *not* to be dwelling in such a state. The only reason the great majority of us do not dwell in *Bodhisattva* is that we have been indoctrinated with a belief system that isolates the individual from her own kind and alienates her from the rest of life.

We can work toward *Bodhisattva* by developing emotional intelligence. This is different from factual, rational, or intellectual intelligence. It is premised on relationship and empathic connections between human beings. We are highly susceptible to being affected by another person's feelings.1 Like viruses, our feelings tend to radiate outward from us and affect everyone around us. In a group situation, the feelings of the person with the biggest presence generates the strongest emotional impact on the rest of the group. A group influenced by a positive emotional contagion experiences greater cohesion, elevated mood, and less conflict.2

Martha Beck writes about this phenomenon in her book *Finding Your Way in a Wild New World*. Rather than having to rely solely on ourselves to elevate our consciousness toward healing, our peers can literally uplift us. Beck writes that a brain whose wave patterns demonstrate calm, relaxation, and a peaceful state of being are able to "pull" other brains into that state.3 This effect, called *entrainment*, occurs whenever two independent systems or signals fall in sync with each other, biologically, musically, or otherwise.4 5 What entrainment reveals to us is that we are hardwired to be aligned with one another.

Similar effects occur in the heart as well. At one level, praying or chanting mantras together can lead the cardiovascular rhythms of a group of people to synchronize.6 Our cardiovascular rhythm has also been shown to align with our breathing rhythm when we think pleasant, loving thoughts.7 Research has also found that the heart rates of romantic partners can synchronize,8 as do the heart rates between a mother and her unborn child.9

What Beck calls *energetic entanglement*10 and researcher Dean Radin calls *entangled minds*11 really amounts to the traditional wisdom of my Blackfoot Elder: *We become what we surround ourselves with.* Understanding how this environmental support for emotional intelligence works can help us in our healing. Knowing that we are going to be emotionally impacted by the people around us and subsequently affected in how our relationship dynamics play out, we can choose to surround ourselves with people who are empowered and who practice healthy relationship behavioral patterns.

What Prevents Immersion Healing

We create boundaries between ourselves and others out of fear and mistrust. If we could trust again, we would have no reason to fear, no reason to establish boundaries to protect ourselves. Those of us who experienced chronic neglect and abuse as children suffer from chronic mistrust as adults. We find it hard to feel safe in relationships, in job situations, and in the world at large. This creates a sad situation for those of us engaging in Immersion healing, which requires camaraderie rooted in trust and respect.

Balance, as I have come to know it, is embracing the unknown and living in trust. I know that sounds like a contradiction, yet it only seems so when we downtrodden humans approach life from a defended-ego perspective. We let go of fearful living when we learn to trust. It gives meaning to life. It creates relationships. It both allows and encourages growth. It sharpens the senses, stimulates the mind, and awakens the feelings. The reason we then feel joy is that we have seen something anew. We are newly open and trusting. Joy, then, is trust, and trust is joy.

TRUST IN WHAT?

In *Part II, #3*, I talk about how trust needs to be informed and selectively placed. How can we do that when here (and in the other two healing steps) it appears as though we are placing blind trust in something that might get us somewhere at some future time? The difference is that here the trust is in ourselves—in the fact that our true self is already healed and just needs to step out into the light. Trusting others really means trusting myself.

Fear is no more than a lack of knowing and, from the Native perspective, trust is knowing. It entails the ability to think and feel as someone else does. It is an innate survival skill used in the hunt to become the animal and know what she is up to. It is also the basis of empathy—the yarn that weaves the fabric of the clan together. When I am able to trust, I have no reason to fear; my ego can relax while I am centered in my Heart-of-Hearts, since by trusting you, I know you. It also means I know *myself*, and I trust my true self to know you.

When we enter this state of being, our dichotomous view of reality leaves us—it is no longer about me or you, Native or non-Native, past or present. I am you, and you are me, and we are all together. We reenter Circle Consciousness, we become attuned to the Hoop of Relations and to all of our relations within the Hoop. It is no longer your Truth or my Truth or her Truth; it is simply Truth.

What can make this vision fraught for some is the reality that in order to immerse ourselves in one experience, we must sometimes distance ourselves from another experience. As uplifting as our new life is becoming, the pangs of our life left behind can be equally devastating. We are simultaneously in a period of rebirth and mourning. Many people feel destabilized during the transition. Trust takes time to build, and new relationships don't come with the warm memories and familiarity that sustain us in times of doubt and insecurity.

Three things we can do in this phase:

1. **Recognize** that feelings of isolation and panic are normal and expected. They are a part of any major transition from old to new.

2. **Support** one another. We are social beings—we are not designed to sustain ourselves alone out in the frontier, even though we needed to venture there alone. This support should be premised on respect. The Maori have a saying, *Never spend time with people who don't respect you*—when we surround ourselves with people who do not respect or support us, we find it difficult to respect and support others.

3. **Trust** in our envisionment of self. When self-doubt looms strong and mighty, it's easy to forget why we left our old life. Even more than that: Most of us end up romanticizing it. The good times take on mythic proportions. Old comforts become necessities. We yearn for the people and places we knew, even though they were not particularly desirable in the past.

A CAVEAT

Be careful of thinking that if you envision your healing environment, you don't have to go out and find one. Use envisioning alone only if there is no other option, or as an adjunct to your Immersion healing experience. The most effective way to turn an envisionment into a reality is to encircle ourselves with people who are living in balance, whether they are leafed or furred or two-legged or four-legged—the more we live in communion with them, the more our light shines, the more our vision grows.

All are sister and brother in the Hoop of Life. Interspecies interactions are heart-stopping in their beauty and intricacy. They are also highly instructional for those of us trying to return to Balance with the natural way. Wild animals cannot live in mistrust. The anxiety would eat them up and they would be making un-centered decisions that would ultimately lead to their demise. Rather than mistrusting Cougar, Deer must trust implicitly in the fact that Cougar is going to get hungry and hunt him. Rather than living his life feeling victimized by the existence of Cougar, Deer can now feel empowered to be who he is and do something about it. Deer is manifesting trust in self.

As part of my healing journey, I trust everyone. The reason is that when I say that I *mistrust* someone:

1. **I have judged him or her,** and in doing so, I have drawn a line between the person and me. There is distance where there could have been relationship.

2. **I have spoken from my ego** rather than from my Heart-of-Hearts, which leaves me in denial of my feelings.

3. **I am externalizing** and placing the blame for my inadequacies on someone else instead of owning the fact that in my relationships, I am as equally involved as the other Person and therefore as equally responsible for the relationship.

Trust empowers me and puts me on the offensive, whereas mistrust victimizes me and puts me on the defensive. Trust stimulates my senses and encourages relationship, whereas mistrust dims my senses and isolates me. Trust encourages perspective, while mistrust narrows focus.

When I am centered, I can trust others as much as I know they are capable of being trusted—and as much as I know I am capable of extending trust. When I am centered and I feel mistrust, I am able to recognize it as unknowing—my unknowing, my fear—and I understand that I am able to overcome it if I am willing to trust. Trust is knowing—I make the only choice available, as it is the natural way: I choose to have relationships based on knowing; I choose to dwell in Trust.

Chapter in a Page

Empowered healing involves immersing ourselves in what we want to become. The same surroundings that formed our state of being can only reinforce it. Healthy and healing people encourage the same in me, and likewise with sick people.

According to Circle Consciousness, we are not just part of our Circle, we *are* our Circle. Life is not about individuals; it is about relationships. This makes healing interactive, premised on connection, and a reflection of our communities. Our real healing partners share our everyday lives and are those who entrench the pattern or help us break it.

Immersion healing requires emotional intelligence and knowing we are highly susceptible to being affected by another person's feelings (emotional contagion). On the other hand, fear and mistrust prevent Immersion healing. We create boundaries between ourselves and others, yet the only way to overcome fearful living is through learning to trust.

Trust needs to be informed and selectively placed. In a deeper sense, though, the trust I am speaking of here is trust in ourselves—in the fact that our true self is already healed and just needs to step out into the light. Trusting others really means knowing that my true self is capable, healed, and radiant. Fear is no more than a lack of knowing and, from the Native perspective, trust is knowing. It is the ability to think and feel as someone else does. Trust is the pretext for joy; in many ways, it *is* joy. In this state, our dichotomous view of reality dissolves—I am you, and you are me, and we are all together now.

As uplifting as our new life is becoming, the pangs of our old life can still be devastating. Three things help to overcome this difficulty:

recognizing that feelings of isolation and panic are normal, supporting and respecting others, and trusting in our envisionment of self. To turn this envisionment into reality, we encircle ourselves with people living in balance, whether they are leafed or furred or two-legged or four-legged. When we surround ourselves with what we want to become, healing occurs as if by osmosis.

Third, Surround Ourselves with What We Want to Become Endnotes

1   Elaine Hatfield, John T. Cacioppo and Richard L. Rapson, *Emotional Contagion* (Cambridge University Press, 1994), 79.

2   Sigal G. Barsade, "The Ripple Effect: Emotional Contagion and Its Influence On Group Behavior," *Administrative Science Quarterly* 47, no. 4 (2002): 644-75.

3   Martha Beck, *Finding Your Way in a Wild New World: Reclaim Your True Nature to Create the Life You Want* (Simon and Schuster, 2011), 112.

4   T.M. Srinivasan, "Entrainment and Coherence in Biology," *International Journal of Yoga* 8, no. 1 (2015): 1.

5   C. Martin, "What is Entrainment? Definition and Applications in Musical Research," *Empir. Musicol. Rev.* 7 (2012): 49-56.

6   Sanjay Kumar, et al., "Meditation on OM: Relevance from Ancient Texts and Contemporary Science," *International Journal of Yoga* 3, no. 1 (2010): 2.

7   William A. Tiller, Rollin McCraty, and Mike Atkinson, "Cardiac Coherence: A New, Noninvasive Measure of Autonomic Nervous System Order," *Alternative Therapies in Health and Medicine* 2, no. 1 (1996): 52-65.

8   Jonathan L. Helm, David Sbarra and Emilio Ferrer, "Assessing Cross-Partner Associations in Physiological Responses Via Coupled Oscillator Models," *Emotion* 12, no. 4 (2012): 748.

9   Peter Van Leeuwen, et al., "Is There Evidence of Fetal-Maternal Heart Rate Synchronization?" *BMC Physiology* 3, no. 1 (2003): 2.

10 Martha Beck, *Finding Your Way in a Wild New World: Reclaim Your True Nature to Create the Life You Want*, 113.

11 Dean Radin, *Entangled Minds: Extrasensory Experiences in a Quantum Reality* (Simon and Schuster, 2009).

Part II

What Keeps Us from It

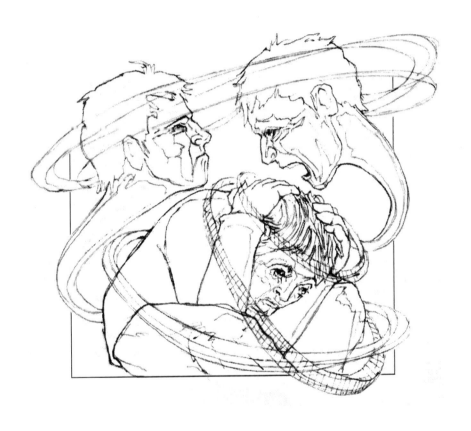

1: We Fight Our Minds

The creation story of the Pima Indians of southern Arizona begins with a Magician, who is known as People Maker. He was baking clay figures in an oven, to populate the new Earth Mother with People of all kinds: winged, four-legged, finned, and leafed People. Except for Coyote People. There was already one: She was the first animal, and she was a mischief-maker who earned an unsavory reputation with the Magician.

When People Maker had to go and gather more firewood, Coyote (who was hiding in the shadows) snuck up to the oven and quickly changed the shape of one of the figures to look like herself. She was lonely, and she knew People Maker would never create a mate for her if she asked.

It took People Maker some time to find enough firewood to bring back, so the figures got over-baked. When he pulled them out of the oven, he was shocked to discover that one of them was a Coyote. "You trickster!" he shouted. "I know you can hear me, and I curse you, for now my life will be tormented many times over by the aggravating antics of not only you but your mate and offspring as well."

However, such was not to be, as the curse had already taken hold. Coyote's mate-to-be, who got over-baked, was too rigid to be a wily Coyote. Instead, he became the first Dog.[1]

We often treat our feelings, behaviors, and habits as if they, too, were made of hard-baked clay: unbending and unchangeable. The reality is just the opposite. We have the capacity to recreate ourselves, and it begins in our minds. Our healing is premised on the very real ability to reprogram our brain by changing how we think and act.

We can better grasp this task by first examining our two-track mind. Then, we explore the role of neural connections in the process of how we change.

One reason many healing approaches are ineffective is that they are not based on how the mind is actually structured and wired. When our healing method is flawed from the start, it inevitably betrays us: We end up fighting our minds and thinking it was entirely our fault. This perspective is not an absolution of personal responsibility in our own healing—it is a reminder that personal responsibility here depends on a healing method that won't turn us against the way we are designed to function psycho-emotionally. When we understand how the mind is structured, we can use that foundational knowledge to our advantage in our healing.

Meet Your Two-Track Brain

Before we take a look at specific behavioral or relationship patterns, it would help to have a basic understanding of brain physiology—the mechanics of our emotional and intellectual functioning. Though we have one mind, it is comprised of two distinct operating systems—or *tracks*, as I refer to them: the limbic and the neocortical. At the root of many of the ways we stay stuck is an imbalance between these two systems.

The limbic system is the base of our emotional functioning and memory. It is the primary system that guides us in our lives: the source of our gut feelings, attractions, repulsions, and all of those urges that are hard to explain or resist. Our limbic mind is the basic animal in us, and there is nothing wrong with it, as first and foremost, we are animals—we share our limbic system with all other higher animals, which includes amphibians, reptiles, birds, and mammals.

The neocortex, on the other hand, is found only in mammals, with the highest neocortex-to-limbic ratio found in humans. The term *neocortex* is Latin for *new bark*, and in common jargon it is our rational brain. Here is the seat of our *shoulds* and *shouldn'ts*, our *planning* and *projecting*—the conscious, studied approach to life. The neocortex evolved as an adjunct to the limbic system, to give it additional range and scope for the complexities of survival and the hunt. In humans, the neocortex developed even further, to give us the capacity for highly coordinated hunts.

When the neocortex and limbic system are working in sync, which is the norm for hunter-gatherers, we are clear in our decisions and motivated in our actions. Much of the stress and anxiety in our lives results from conflict between the neocortex and the limbic system. Contemporary humans often receive different messages from each, as in, "I'd like to eat this piece of apple pie, but I know it's made with lots of sugar and hydrogenated oil."

What we are left with is a present-day version of the parable of the Garden of Eden—the fall from paradise—or what I call the *Adam and Eve Syndrome*: There is the delicious homemade apple pie, and there is the thou-shalt-not-eat-the-apple-pie. We have pitted our natural impulses and modern injunctions against one another. We deny ourselves the pie and yearn for it nonetheless; or we indulge in it, chastising ourselves all the while, and then the pie somehow tastes bitter, as if it were made with that rotten apple from the previous chapter.

Rather than balancing the limbic system and the neocortex—our feeling self and our thinking self—we allow one, then the other, to dominate. When the limbic system dominates, we become intuitive, sensitive, and perceptive beings who act based on feeling rather than reason. On the other hand, when the neocortex dominates, we can be dispassionate, highly efficient, and productive, although we also tend to be self-possessed and antisocial. When we are running with both systems in sync, we can be passionate and engaging as well as productive and reflective—the way our hunter-gatherer ancestors were.

Our basic needs and motivations are not going to change—they are set for life—to try to change them would simply worsen the fight in our minds. This book cannot guarantee your ability to work out the balance between your core and cerebral selves, your feeling and your thinking selves—rather, it helps you see how the bulk of our relationship struggles are rooted in the classic conflict between these selves. And most importantly, it offers tools for reengaging the two selves and reestablishing a working relationship.

Contemporary healing methods tend to aggravate the fight in our minds by blaming the two-track mind for having two tracks. The clinical method often begins with an evaluation that identifies the problem as something like *You overanalyze,* or *You act impulsively.* This approach problematizes the human mind from the get-go. It overlooks the wholeness beneath these evaluations: that we are, by nature, highly reflective and passionate creatures—the one quality does not exclude the other. These injunctions falsely pit the two sides of our mind against each other instead of honoring their complementarity.

Imagine what a difference it would make to our healing if we abandoned the trope of our thinking self *versus* our feeling self—if we began by embracing that we are thinking *and* feeling beings. When we attack one quality or the other or see them as in competition, we attack the foundation of our core self instead of our core problem. It is as if we blame our nose for smelling the rotten apple in our fridge—we're not looking deeply enough. We focus too much on the things that cannot change and, in the process, forget about what actually can.

Neural Connections and How They Work

There is a Zen saying that the mind is a wonderful servant and a terrible master. Contemporary findings in neuroscience add some nuance to this adage. Specifically, the various neural connections in our brain help determine the ways our mind either serves us or rules us.

To start, the brain does not distinguish between positive and negative input. No matter what we think or feel about something, if we expose ourselves to it, we are establishing a neural connection. While we cannot determine all of our neural input, we can choose some of it. Here is where we begin to change. We have an active role in the patterns our mind establishes and those related behaviors—it all begins with neural connections.

The following are five key points to remember about neural connections as they relate to our healing:

1. **Neurons that fire together, wire together.** Neurons are specialized cells that transmit nerve impulses. When one set of neurons brings us the image of a Bird and another set of neurons imports the song of the same Bird, these two sets of neurons link.[2] Once the link is formed, we just have to hear the song in order to associate it with the image, and vice versa.[3]

2. **Neurons that fire apart, wire apart.** This prevents us from seeing a Bird one moment, hearing the song of another Bird the next moment, and wiring the two together. This gap also allows us to reprogram our brain.[4]

3. **Neurons out of sync fail to link.** We can read in a book about a particular Bird singing a particular song, yet this is only an intellectual understanding. When we hear the song, we have to sort through our memory files—an intellectual process—to link it with the image of the Bird we retained from the book.[5]

1. **New experiences add new neural connections,** the potential for which is nearly limitless. Repetition and sameness

neurologically reinforce routines, which make us predictable and reliable. We must cultivate new learning opportunities and reach outside our comfort zone, or this predictability and reliability turn into stagnancy.[6]

2. **We learn and unlearn simultaneously.** The brain is designed for novelty, so it has the ability to respond quickly to new stimuli. Old neural connections that limit our abilities are erased automatically during the formation of new links that expand our potential. To keep the mind adaptable, it is important to continually learn and experience new things.[7]

Neural connections underpin our brain's ability to recognize our world and build patterns, some of which may contribute to our dysfunctional lives. Yet neural connections are not monoliths—repetition makes them stronger, while new experiences disrupt them. We are creatures of habit *and* we are adaptable. Each experience we have can be used to reinforce old patterns or support new ones.

If you were to listen to your least favorite song continuously on repeat, it would become imprinted in the front of your conscious mind. With every repetition, the lyrics, rhythm, and beat are further ingrained, much to your chagrin. How do you dislodge this song? By deciding to stop hitting the repeat button and by choosing to listen to new music. When you stop exposing yourself to the unpleasant song, you weaken its neural connection. When you expose yourself to new lyrics, rhythms, and beats, those new connections form, then strengthen.

Blaming the neural connections themselves would simply be fighting our mind. Yes, they are part of the problem of the awful song stuck in our head—yet they are also part of the solution since they represent the possibility of a more beautiful song on our mind. When we're able to see our mind as our ally, we can use its functions to our advantage in our healing.

A POINT ABOUT MUSIC

Continuous noise lowers intelligence.[8, 9] Do you know all those tunes that keep rolling around in your head? They are monopolizing neural connections that could be used for other things. And it's not just old songs—background noise of any sort clogs the brain with largely useless information.

Chapter in a Page

Our one mind is comprised of two tracks: the limbic and the neocortical. An imbalance between these two systems causes us to stagnate. First, the limbic system is the base of our emotional functioning and memory, guiding us and generating gut feelings, attractions, and repulsions. The neocortex, or *rational brain*, is the seat of our planning and projecting. It evolved to enhance the limbic system for the complexities of survival and the hunt.

When the two tracks are working in sync—the norm for hunter-gatherers—we generate clear decisions and motivated actions. Contemporary humans rarely balance these systems, instead allowing one or the other to prevail. When the limbic system dominates, we become intuitive, sensitive, and perceptive beings who act based on feeling rather than reason. When the neocortex dominates, we are dispassionate, highly efficient, and productive, yet also self-possessed and antisocial.

Contemporary healing methods often blame our two-track mind for our problems, by saying we either think or feel *too much*. We must abandon the trope of our thinking self *versus* our feeling self and embrace both. When we see them as competing, we attack the foundation of our core self instead of addressing our core problem.

A Zen saying states that the mind is a wonderful servant and a terrible master. Our neural connections determine how our mind either serves or rules us. They allow our brain to recognize our world and build patterns, some of which may be dysfunctional. Yet neural connections are not monoliths—repetition makes them stronger, while new experiences disrupt them. Each experience either reinforces old patterns (habits) or supports new ones (adaptations).

The brain does not distinguish between positive and negative input—if we expose ourselves to something, we establish a neural connection with it. While we cannot determine all of our neural input, we can choose some of it. Here is where we begin to change.

1: We Fight Our Minds Endnotes

1   Richard Erdoes and Alfonso Ortiz, "How Mosquitoes Came to Be," *American Indian Myths and Legends* (Pantheon, 1984), 192-93.

2   Deann Ware, Ph.D., "Neurons that Fire Together Wire Together," *Psychologists Guide to Emotional Wellbeing,* last modified 8 October 2013, accessed 13 October 2020, http://www.dailyshoring.com/neurons-that-fire-together-wire-together/.

3   Ibid.

4   Laurie Bartels, "Neuroplasticity and the Brain that Changes Itself," *Sharp Brains: Tracking Health and Wellness Applications of Brain Science,* last modified 12 November 2008, accessed 13 October 2020, http://sharpbrains.com/blog/2008/11/12/neuroplasticity-and-the-brain-that-changes-itself/.

5   Ibid.

6   Dr. Pascale Michelon, "Brain Plasticity: How Learning Changes Your Brain," *Sharp Brains: Tracking Health and Wellness Applications of Brain Science*, Feb. 26, 2008, http://sharpbrains.com/blog/2008/02/26/brain-plasticity-how-learning-changes-your-brain/.

7   Andrea Kuszewski, "You Can Increase Your Emotional Intelligence: 5 Ways to Maximize Your Cognitive Potential," *Scientific American,* last modified 7 March 2011, accessed 13 October 2020, http://blogs.scientificamerican.com/guest-blog/2011/03/07/you-can-increase-your-intelligence-5-ways-to-maximize-your-cognitive-potential/.

8   Mohammad Javad Jafari, "The Effect of Noise Exposure on Cognitive Per-
    formance and Brain Activity Patterns," *Open Access Maced J. Med. Sci.* 7,
    no. 17 (2019): 2924-31.

9   Soo-young Bhang, et al., "Comparing Attention and Cognitive Function in
    School Children Across Noise Conditions: A Quasi-Experimental Study,"
    Psychiatry Investigation 15, no. 6 (2018): 620-27.

2: We Resist Our Natures

Our core self has a personality, which we can refer to as our *core nature.* It is composed of three things: our archetypal energy, genetics-based character traits, and gender role. We have already discussed how, for our personal healing journeys to be fruitful, we must acknowledge the structure and functioning of our minds. We must also be cognizant of our core natures, or else our healing ceases to be personal. Once that happens, it is unlikely for any healing to actually take place.

To others, our core nature manifests as a combination of our basic worldview and the role we play in community. It is an expression of our individuality in the context of our relationships with others. When we understand our core nature, we can better discern our healing needs and the form that our journey should take. In the introduction I mentioned that the only person you need to trust is yourself—this chapter explores just who that person is.

The Role of the Guardian, Nurturer, and Voice Archetypes

A pack of Wolves has ventured beyond their home territory. They travel cautiously and on alert. Normally they would stay well within their range, where they know the terrain and feel secure. However, they need to find more food for the fast-growing pups, who have just gotten old enough to travel with the pack.

Approaching a willow-rich river bottom, they intuit the scent of a Moose and fan out to better intercept his trail. The pack's matron stops abruptly. She sniffs the air, then the ground. The stench of a wounded Moose tickles her nostrils. She quickly determines his direction of travel, and without uttering a sound, she turns to trail him down toward the river.

Attuned to each other's movements, the hunters pick up on their matron's actions and fall in behind her. They move swiftly yet deliberately, so as not to lose the scent or alert the animal before catching up with him. Surprise is key to a successful hunt. The Voice pair, who coordinates the pack, is right at her heels. The stable, mild-mannered aunts and uncles take the middle of the column with the pups. Meanwhile, the wary individuals with sharper senses flank the pack and bring up the rear.

"Wouw!" yelps the last of them as he spins around, lowers his head and tail, and shrinks slowly backward. The entire pack freezes in their tracks and the Voice couple sprints to the back of the line. With hackles raised, teeth bared, and thunder rumbling from their pulsing chests, they take commanding positions to defend the pack.

Facing them across the small opening is the pack on whose territory they are infringing. In both camps, tension screams as the pups instinctively pull together, the nannies surround them, and the wolves on the side and in the rear shy back, taking positions at strategic spots around the periphery to pick up on any surprises. Without losing focus on the threat, the coordinator pair remains acutely keyed in to the wolves on the periphery. The pair, like set traps, are ready to shift position or rush in the instant they are needed. All that matters to the pack is the safety of the pups—their future. The calm, stable presence of the nannies keeps the wolflings quiet and contained during the standoff.

The infringing pack, knowing they have overstepped their bounds and feeling uneasy because of it, take their cue from one of the elder pack members and slowly back away in retreat. Too fast, and they would trigger a chase by the other pack; too slow, and the other pack would swarm across the buffer zone, and battle would rage. Pups would surely die. To discourage a rush from the other pack, the front pair maintains an imposing stance while stepping gingerly backward. The flanking wolves take outer positions and scout ahead to catch any surprise attack and chart the safest way back to their home turf.

How the Archetypes Manifest

Just as the movement of the pack is fluid, so are the manifestations of the three archetypes: Guardian, Nurturer, and Voice. They are not concrete roles so much as *patterns of energy* that emanate from their limbic systems. At times these energies intersect, as when an animal of one archetype is called upon to serve by assuming another archetypal role. Nonetheless, each animal exhibits an energy pattern that corresponds to one of the three archetypes.

The aunts, uncles, and nannies in the Wolf story are Nurturers: They serve their pack through their tenderness and orientation to caretaking. The matron and the wolves flanking the pack are Guardians. Their role is to keep perspective on the scene and be attuned to the pack's vulnerability. The coordinator pair are Voices. They occupy the front of the pack and speak on its behalf.

We can understand the intertwined experience of the archetypes the same way we understand the harmony of our sensory organs. Our eyes are the Guardian; our hands, the Nurturer; and our mouth and ears, the Voice. Each serves a distinct role, yet there may be times when we communicate with our eyes or see with our hands. Although the archetypal role can be fluid and interchangeable, the purpose served by each role is specific. Indeed, even if we are seeing with our hands, we still identify the experience as one of *seeing*.

As with a Wolf pack, the archetypes work in balance with one another in our human communities to help them survive and thrive. The synergy is so vital that a person of one archetype is powerless without those of the other archetypes around her to provide context, support, and nourishment.

The story of the Wolf pack illustrates the three archetypes as verbs rather than nouns. In my own experience with living as a member of a Wolf pack, I learned that the unique way each archetype manifested in relation to the pack gave me another example for how to be fully present and engaged with life. Together, the archetypal interaction provided me a living metaphor for how to be open and accepting of all that is. By assuming an interactive archetypal role in the pack, the wolves showed me that what is around me is merely an extension of what is inside me—which is a key to the personal healing journey.

Archetype and Culture

In our society, it can be difficult to discern one's archetype. We create our identities by distinguishing ourselves from our group, so that we can stand alone as a distinct entity. This runs counter to how archetypal energies function. As we saw in the Wolf story, our archetype indicates our role in serving *our clan*, not ourselves. Our archetype manifests as an experience of relationship rather than individualism.

To return to the metaphor of the senses: We could remove the hands, eyes, and tongue to grant each of the senses complete autonomy, as is the way of our culture. Each would then no longer have to answer to the others. Yet each alone would struggle to survive with such one-dimensional sensory input. The same is true of each of us when we function alone. In order to serve our people and be cared for ourselves, we need to function interactively with individuals of all archetypes, just as with the Wolf pack.

Individualist-based independence (and the resultant struggle) is alien to Traditional Peoples. They function in a circle of *inter*dependence, defining individual self in terms of relationship rather than ego. They transcend the false struggle of *autonomy versus immersion* to understand that the individual achieves actualization and expression through immersion and serving the group.

Who we are as people is independent of our institutions and how they affect the manifestation of archetypal roles. When we sit down together around the hearth or enter the woods and merge with our plant and animal Relations, we rejoin the continuum where the archetypes are alive and well. Understanding the archetypal energy resonating in you can help you access part of your core self—the base of your healing. When you can better recognize your own archetypal energy, you understand how to enter into relationship with others.

The Guardian Archetype

Guardians have the ability to keep perspective, be unobtrusive yet keenly present, and serve in any archetypal role as needed. They are the Voices' eyes and ears and the Nurturers' extended reach. Serving as message bearers, emissaries, advisors, scouts, and protectors, they are able to maintain perspective and act dispassionately in dynamic and high-stress situations.

People who display Attention Deficit Disorder (ADD) characteristics would be apt for the role of the Guardian in hunter-gatherer cultures. ADD symptoms, such as the inability to stay focused or follow through on something, turn out to be desirable Guardian characteristics. One of the Guardian's roles is to be ever alert and keep tabs on what is going on all around. If she were to get lost in a project, important occurrences could escape her attention.

Another Guardian role in traditional cultures is to notice things that need attention, so that the Nurturers and Voices can follow up on them. This keeps the Guardians free to continue their vital function of being on watch.

In our day, Guardian behavior is often seen in team sports, where there is fast-paced action, coordinated interaction, and the need to maintain perspective on multiple dynamics occurring simultaneously. For many people, team sports are the only venue for Guardian-like training and experiencing clan-style archetypal relationship.

The Nurturer Archetype

Nurturers naturally seek to create space around them that supports soul-to-soul communication. Just being in the presence of a Nurturer can often feel like being in a sacred space or enveloped in maternal energy. These individuals serve their clan or community by strengthening and healing interpersonal bonds. In doing so, they hold the clan together and ensure its long-term survival.

In times past, when we lived as clanspeople (and in this day to some degree), Nurturers were the ones to welcome new clan members, recognize their archetypes and talents, and help them integrate in ways that they could best serve and feel personally fulfilled. Nurturers also have a knack for tending to ancestral relationships as well as to relationships with those yet to arrive or be born. Other roles they played were helping people choose mates and tend to relationship issues—services that are sadly lacking and dearly missed in our contemporary culture.

Although Nurturers may not typically demonstrate the commanding, up-front presence of Voices, they are nonetheless capable of stepping forward when necessary. At the root of the Nurturer archetype is sensitivity and the ability to perceive and respond with empathy and gentleness.

The Voice Archetype

Plenty-Coups, Chief of the Crows, is remembered for his ability as a leader to create consensus, maintain perspective on options, and garner the loyalty of his people even amid detractors and criticism.[1] Each of these accomplishments points to his Voice archetype.

Voices exhibit the receptivity, understanding, synthesizing ability, and charisma needed to process raw feedback, coordinate, and inspire. They know how to put the right people in the right place.

We who have not experienced the organic, synergistic interplay of the archetypes tend to magnify and standardize the role of the Voice.

Hence, we have presidents, dictators, team captains, gang leaders, and so on. Leadership in Native cultures is based on the people deferring to particular individuals *in particular instances*. Whom is deferred to at any one time is based on contextual considerations such as knowledge and skill level in a specific area, along with the ability to convey what is needed, rather than simply dominance or entitlement.

In our culture, it is common to see Voice energy distorted into power addiction, deception, pontificating, demagogy, and bullying. This typically self-righteous, aggressive, subjugating approach keeps our hierarchical system running. Those with the most strongly distorted Voice energies are the ones most likely to advance their careers to high positions in politics, business, or religion, and they are commonly considered to be the most successful people in our society.

In Traditional cultures, the Voice mirrors the needs of the group, whatever they might be. She stands simultaneously at the fore and in the background. She knows that for the clan to flourish, each individual needs to flourish.

When complacency settles in, the Voice injects chaos into the mix as a precursor to change. A small change orchestrated by the Voice can send a ripple through the group that brings forth a transformation, so it is important that every ear be attuned to the Voice's conducting. Although either Guardians, Nurturers, or Voices can sniff out what is off-kilter and needs to be addressed, it is the Voice who usually initiates the corresponding action.

Initiating a course of action is based on good communication, which is based on the ability to hear all perspectives and see all the needs, and from there, discerning in which direction to go. Whereas Guardians are cautious and questioning (as their role is to be on alert for disturbance and vulnerability), Voices are confident and definitive. They must be, in order to effectively lead the clan on a particular course of action or to negotiate with another clan.

Gender and Archetype

There is some general confusion around the relationship between archetypes and gender. Foremost is the tendency for people to see *nurturing* and *providing* as one and the same. Although nurturing is providing, and providing is nurturing, the roles are gender-distinct, with nurturing being feminine and providing being masculine.

Gender differences in behavior are common throughout the plant and animal kingdoms. In only a tiny handful of animal species are male and female offspring raised differently, yet virtually all of them display specialized gender behaviors. Humans are one of those few species who tend to give gender-specific attention to their children. Yet we need to be careful about assuming that we have a nurture-versus-nature situation here, as in theory, it could just as well be nurture magnifying nature.

Generally speaking, the evolution of gender roles goes something like this: Women are most often the gatherers and men are the hunters, with women oriented to the hearth and men drawn to scouting. With our early domestication, women turned to gardening and men to herding. The next stage found women spinning and men handling the draft animals. Setting aside the question of male and female capacities, what we know is that men and women served distinct evolutionary roles.[2] In terms of our core nature, the gender roles are not hierarchical. Much like the archetypes, they simply reflect our personal energy and the ways we may best serve our community.

Gender is a key factor in how our minds evolved and function, so it ought to be considered in recognizing who we are as psycho-emotional beings and thus how it might also affect our woundedness. With that said, it is only *one* factor. The archetypal energies can manifest in a person of any gender.

Are You a Stay-at-Homer or Trailblazer?

Another way we resist our natures is with two distinct, genetically based character traits found in our species, which I refer to colloquially as *stay-at-homer* and *trailblazer*. Roughly one out of three of us is a stay-at-homer, with the same ratio being trailblazers. The remaining third of us fall somewhere in the middle. Knowledge of the two traits helps make sense of the constant struggle in cultures between liberals and conservatives, and revolutionaries and reactionaries.

As with the two-track mind and the archetypes, understanding which character trait we identify with helps us see that much of our inner struggle with values and expectations actually turns out to be us fighting our own nature.

The stay-at-homers are the ones that keep the family farm or business going for generations. They're involved in community affairs, they're loyal to their mates, and they thrive on time-honored traditions. Here you find our model citizens and pillars of stability in all areas of life. And here you also find religious ultraconservatives, cultural isolationists, and racists.

The trailblazers, who are the polar opposites of the stay-at-homers, are marked by a penchant for the unknown, always with an eye out for what's over the next hill. Our explorers, adventurers, and creative people fall into this category. They like variety in their lives, whether it be with projects, diet, or sexual partners. Craving stimulation, they are drawn to extreme sports and take risks in many areas of their lives. Their adventurism has its downside as well—a high percentage of criminals and drug and alcohol abusers carry the trailblazer gene.

Origin of These Two Traits

For 97 percent of Homo sapiens' existence, we have lived as hunter-gatherers. Every day we relied on our wits to keep us safe, comfortable, and nourished. Those needs can be provided in either of two ways:

- Sticking with tried-and-true sources and methodologies, or

- Finding new sources and methodologies.

In other words, we satiate needs by being a stay-at-homer or a trailblazer. Even though the approaches appear to be diametrically opposed, they each have their advantages when time and circumstance favor them, so in the long run, they average out to be equally successful—which is why an equal number of us have a genetic predisposition for each group.

Let's take a look at how the scenarios favoring each group might have played out. Imagine it is 30,000 years ago and you are living with your clan. It is a time of drought, and the water hole you rely on for your drinking water—as well as for the animals you hunt when they come to drink—is drying up. What do you do to ensure the survival of your people?

About one-third of you want to stay right where you are. Even though your water hole is shrinking, your reasoning is that it is a known entity, so why risk leaving it and maybe ending up with nothing?

Around the same number of you want to head out, actually for the same reason some of your kin want to stay: Your water hole is a known entity. However, your perspective is that there has to be more water out there somewhere, so let's find it and increase our odds of survival.

Which approach is going to save the clan? If the drought is short-lived, your water hole might sustain you until the rains return. If you leave for greener pastures and find none, the clan might perish. However, if the drought persists and the clan stays at the water hole, you could become so dehydrated by having to ration the rapidly disappearing water that you wouldn't be able to move to a more favorable location even if one was found. Your trailblazers, on the other hand, would have left early enough to find that favorable site and guide the rest of the clan to it. Or they may have dragged themselves to their deaths out on a landscape even more parched than the one they left.

If clans functioned by majority rule, it would be all or nothing—the entire clan could either survive or perish, depending upon whether the stay-at-homers or the trailblazers swung the majority. The more likely scenario is that the clan would split, increasing the odds of at least half of the clan surviving, and possibly the entire clan. Pressure on the water hole would be reduced by half, and the trailblazers might find water for themselves elsewhere. In this way, similar to the two-track mind, although these two character traits—being a stay-at-homer or a trailblazer—are opposites, they can coexist without conflict.

Exercise: Which One Are You?

This story is a metaphor for experiences in your life. Relive one of your own experiences and notice which role you played: trailblazer, stay-at-homer, or in the middle. Is that your typical role? This question could help you choose the healing approach best suited for you.

Here are some generalizations to help you determine which group you fall into:

* Stay-at-homers are tidy and well organized; trailblazers are disheveled.

* Timeliness is a stay-at-homer quality; trailblazers, who tend to cram as much into the moment as possible, are often late.

* Stay-at-homers like to finish one project before starting another, while trailblazers usually have several projects going at once.

* Doers are stay-at-homers; dreamers are trailblazers.

* Long-lasting marriages are the norm for stay-at-homers, while trailblazers have multiple relationships.

* Saving money and buying insurance is the way of the stay-at-homer, whereas gambling, playing the stock market, and trusting in tomorrow is the trailblazer's way.

WHERE DO SHY PEOPLE FIT?

Many assume that outgoing and assertive people are trailblazers, while reclusive, retiring types are stay-at-homers. It turns out that neither shyness nor being outgoing has much to do with the two character types. A shy person could just as easily be a trailblazer as a stay-at-homer, and the same is true with a highly social person. A shy person might be a solo trailblazer, while a stay-at-homer could be a socialite.

Although archetypal energies manifest in trailblazer and stay-at-home character traits, much like gender, they are not deterministic. Often it is assumed that all Voices are trailblazers and all Nurturers are stay-at-homers, when in fact, evolutionary reasons preclude such a thing. Returning to our story above, if all Voices in the clan were trailblazers and took off to find a new water hole, only to fail and perish, that would leave the clan entirely without the vital coordinating abilities that Voices provide. Thus, some Voices are trailblazers, while others are stay-at-homers. This fluidity allows for each to remain present in the clan to ensure its survival, especially if they need to split up.

Our Character and Our Healing

Unfortunately, in their present-day incarnations, both the stay-at-homers and the trailblazers carry the burden of cultural prejudices. We treat stay-at-homers like closed-minded stick-in-the-muds, while on the other hand, we idolize them as the God, mom, and apple pie backbone of our culture. Meanwhile, we belittle trailblazers as self-centered or renegade idealists, yet we romanticize the images of the pioneer and the rebel without a cause.

These prejudices prevent us from fully embracing whichever of these traits corresponds to our character. Then this hesitation, in turn, disrupts our healing. Glorifying or denigrating the stay-at-homers or the trailblazers transforms each into a rigid, all-encompassing identity. We can identify with our innate character trait without identifying ourselves in our entirety as that trait. Much like our archetype or our gender, it is one indicator that helps us gain a better understanding of our core self.

Now let's take a look at how knowledge of your character trait can influence your healing. The rule of thumb I go by is that nature overrides nurture easier than nurture overrides nature. Consider the following: An adventurous child who is reined in might be forced to act outwardly like a stay-at-homer; however, he/she very likely manifests his/her nature by becoming broody and rebellious. It is much easier to reshape our method to work with our character traits than vice versa.

Let's say you're a stay-at-homer and want to choose a healing approach. You're considering one that you see holding a lot of prom- ise, yet it scares you, as you don't know anyone who has tried it and you would have to go it alone. It may be time to listen to your fear, which is telling you that with your innate psychological makeup, you would do better with a healing approach involving other people or one with incremental steps that feel comfortable to you. Otherwise, you would risk hurting yourself by overriding your fear and forcing an approach upon yourself that is incompatible with who you are.

On the other hand, if you were a trailblazer, you would be drawn to something new that holds a lot of potential. Along with the excite- ment of exploring the unknown, you are hardwired to take the risk in hopes of reaping the greater reward. Your character trait can help you be more intentional about seeking experimental, independent, or fast-paced approaches to healing.

Whichever character trait defines you—or if you fall somewhere in between—the more aware you are of your innate characteristics and how they affect you, the more rapid and effective your healing can be. Your self-knowledge helps you discern what kind of healing approach works with, not against, your core self.

Chapter in a Page

Our core self has a personality, or core nature, comprised of three things: our archetype, a gender role, and a genetics-based character trait. Knowing our core nature enables personal and effective healing. The core self is the only person you need to trust.

The three archetypes—Guardian, Nurturer, and Voice—are *patterns of energy* emanating from our limbic system. Each person's energy corresponds to an archetype and requires balance in a group: Other archetypes provide context, support, and nourishment.

Our archetype determines how we can best serve our community. Guardians keep perspective, organize, and lead. They are charismatic and often act as message bearers and emissaries. Nurturers create space for soul-to-soul communication and connection. They preserve and heal interpersonal bonds, holding the clan together. Voices are attuned to clan members' perspectives; they create consensus and direct the clan on a course of action, including negotiations with other clans.

The archetypes manifest in any gender. Still, throughout human evolution, men and women served distinct roles. The question becomes whether you have the brain of a nurturer or a provider, i.e., the traditional roles of females or males, respectively.

Finally, our core nature also exhibits a genetically based character trait: the stay-at-homer or the trailblazer. Any population is roughly equal parts stay-at-homer, trailblazer, and those in the middle. Stay-at-homers are the traditionalists and conservatives. Trailblazers are the pioneers and adventurers. Societies need both to survive. Each has its advantages, and in the long run, they average out to be equally successful.

This character trait can help determine the appropriate method and pace of healing for someone. Stay-at-homers are best served by involving others or tracking incremental accomplishments. Trailblazers prefer an experimental, independent, or fast-paced approach. When we understand our core nature, we can engage in healing that works with it, not against it.

2: We Resist Our Natures Endnotes

1 Frank B. Linderman, *Plenty-Coups, Chief of the Crows* (Bison Books, 2002), x-15.

2 Helen Fisher, *The First Sex: The Natural Talents of Women and How They Are Changing The World* (Ballantine Books, 2010), 159.

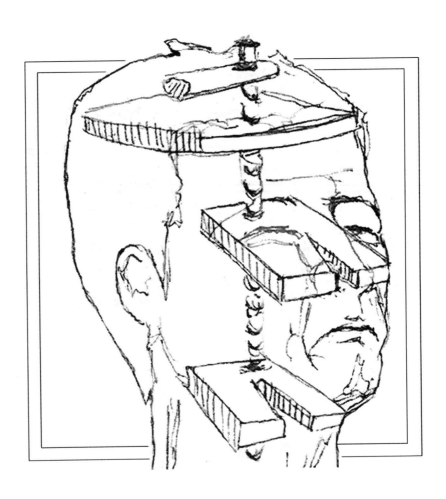

3: We Hang On to Old Beliefs

When the Greek philosopher Diogenes witnessed a young beggar drinking water from his cupped palms, Diogenes immediately cast away the only bowl in his possession so he could rid himself of all superfluous things.[1] Just as he already possessed what he needed to quench his thirst—his hands—we already possess what we need for our personal healing: our core self.

Yet, we too carry the burden of Diogenes' bowl, as many of our contemporary beliefs about healing divert our attention away from our innate capacity to heal. As this chapter reveals, we must mimic Diogenes and cast away some of what we have received as contemporary wisdom. We need to expose some of the lies we have been taught to live by.

This is where personal responsibility in our healing begins—by examining our preconceived beliefs and being willing to deconstruct them. When a house is built on a shaky foundation, its walls soon crack, doors and windows get pinched in their frames, floors buckle, and basements leak. The same is true of our lives: When they are based on erroneous beliefs and principles, they falter.

Our journey forward is not about our parents, our upbringing, or our inner child—it is about *us*, in this moment. It takes great courage to stand on our own, naked to our past, free of both pretense and blame. When we are unadorned and unburdened by illusion and belief, we can begin to build anew.

The Beginner's Mind

Whether we drink from replenishing waters using our cupped hands or a bowl, each has one thing in common—emptiness. Our vessel must first be empty in order to receive. In much the same way, we must approach our personal healing with emptiness, which, in this context, takes the form of abandoning our old beliefs about healing. This first step is akin to the Zen concept of *beginner's mind*, which the following story illustrates.

There was once an Elder who was a breeder of magnificent bulls. They were known for their majesty and for the fire in their eyes. It was the time in his life to travel and share what he had gained, so he offered his herd for sale

Three people expressed interest. This posed a dilemma, as the Elder wanted to both be fair to them and make sure that his animals would receive the best of care. He decided to ask each of them three questions:

"What would you feed the herd?"

"I would buy the best greens and the sweetest hay," answered the first.

"I would provide them with a verdant pasture of life-giving herbs and wildflowers," the second replied.

"I am not sure," responded the third.

"And what would you do if a bull attacked you?" asked the Elder.

"I would shoot him on the spot."

"I would run and jump over the fence."

The third man answered only, "I do not know."

"And my last question," spoke the breeder: "What if the barn caught fire and the bulls could not escape?"

"I would chop a hole in the side of the barn and risk my life to save them—they are too precious to burn to death."

"I would ring the bell for the villagers to come and help put out the fire, and at the same time I would say a prayer for the bulls' safety."

Again, the third person answered, "I do not know what I would do."

The two other men chuckled under their breaths.

"I will consider your answers," stated the Elder. "Please come tomorrow at sunrise, and you will have my decision."

When the three men arrived, the Elder asked the three if they would give the same answers today to his questions that they gave yesterday.

They each replied, "Yes."

"I will then entrust my herd to the one who knows nothing. Two of you are already filled with beliefs. That would make it hard to teach you how to care for the herd, as you think you already know what to do, even in an emergency. To be a Master is to be empty: to know and believe in nothing. It is how the greatest Master remains the greatest student. And that is why he who has no answers will be able to listen to the bulls, and they will teach him how to care for them."

It came to pass that the man who knew nothing became renowned for his majestic fire-eyed bulls and his skill in handling them. And in time, like his predecessor, he became known across the land as a wise Elder.

Finding Wisdom in Every Moment

Our healing process cannot avoid slip-ups or errors. However, approaching it with beginner's mind helps us see that within each of these pitfalls are eye-openers, teachers, and opportunities. In essence, there are no accidents, and there is no such thing as wasted time. It is only wasted if we choose to let it be so.

What we call *bad luck* and *fate* are merely our inability to bring what is going on internally into our consciousness so that we can work with it. We become victimized, either blaming others or attributing our circumstances to some external cause. We give ourselves permission to surrender instead of stepping into the moment.

If one were to ask a Native or member of a Traditional culture about mistakes, failures, or accidents, she would likely reply that they do not exist. Hawaiian elder Kaili'ohe Kame'ekua, who lived in the 1800s, put it this way: "We were taught from the time we could understand, that there are no accidents. All things happen for a reason. We may not know what the reason is at the moment, but to always be happy even for misfortune, for with it comes some wisdom that we could not have had otherwise."[2] One of my favorite bits of folk wisdom is the German *Ein guter Stolperer fällt nicht—A good stumbler falleth not.*[3]

If the simplest thing we can do to grow in wisdom is to admit we're fools, we'd be fools not to. Next, we turn our attention to specific examples of old beliefs about healing that do us more harm than good. Once we're aware of what they are, we can thank them for the wisdom we've learned from them and continue on our journey.

Belief 1: "The Past Is Dead"

Many of us live according to the past—we harbor shame about past events and try to atone for them, or we become victims. At the same time, when we try to put the past to rest or ignore it, we are trying to live in denial of who we are. Yet, fundamentally, we are our past: Without it we would not be who we are. To love and accept ourselves, we need to learn to embrace our past.

Our healing comes from recognizing that our lives can be *informed* by the past without being directed by it. In fact, we *can direct* the past. If we shaped it initially, we can reshape it. If I'm alive, my past is alive. Since I am my past, changing how I perceive my past changes my present: It changes me. Let me illustrate how this works with an example of a past event where I saw myself as a victim.

Version 1 of the past: Susan, my wife, left me for another man. I was abandoned; she cheated on me. I was good to her; I didn't deserve this. I did everything for her, gave her everything she wanted. I can't understand why it happened. I must be a real loser.

Version 2 of the past: Susan finally had enough—she packed up and left. I kept blaming her for our troubles; I wouldn't go to counseling. I wouldn't look at what I might be doing to create the situation. Her leaving helped to wake me up from my coma. It may be too late for our relationship, but it's not too late for me. Now Susan has a chance to heal, a chance for the life she deserves. I admire her for having the courage to break our pattern, and I am grateful to her for giving me this opportunity to heal.

Had I allowed the first version to remain the singular experience of my past, I would simply be reinforcing a dysfunctional pattern in my life—remember, what we feed grows. The second version is the same past—with the same people, events, and outcome—yet my changed perspective supports my healing. Every time I tell the story, whether to myself or others, I am breaking my pattern in dysfunctional relationships and creating a potential to grow, heal, and perhaps have healthy relationships.

We can also apply this thinking to the stories we tell ourselves regarding negativity or even—yes, shame. When we settle for labeling an experience as negative, we deprive ourselves of a valuable opportunity to heal. Shame, as flushed and pained as it leaves us in the moment, can also serve as an awareness-raising exercise. There is wisdom in every moment—and while that awareness doesn't erase the pain, it allows us to redirect it in a way that serves our healing, not our woundedness.

I am my own *potential* perfection. It is me and only me who can grow into my fully actualized self, and negativity and shame help get me there—if I choose to allow them to. In order to be perfect, I must be imperfect. In order to grow, I must be vulnerable. And in order to see with perspective, I must act with a beginner's mind—I must be as a question, willing to be undefended and grow. Shame is one of the best tools I know of to fulfill every one of those needs.

To avoid or deny negative and shameful experiences is to come from a place of illusory strength and self-assuredness. To deny them is as futile as denying the past. I would ostensibly be creating a boundary to protect myself from the pangs of shame, whereas in actuality, I would be blocking myself from the awarenesses and possibilities that could come from it.

The reason shame can be such a powerful tool for healing is not for what it brings us directly (which is typically feelings of being damaged and undeserving), but rather what it sprang from. Addressing shame itself is merely treating a symptom of deep woundedness. The symptom becomes a beacon to identify and shed light on that woundedness when we have the awareness and courage to embrace our shame for what it truly is.

TRUE OR FALSE

Just as there is wisdom in every moment, there is truth even in the things our culture has taught us to treat as lies. Our personal healing involves looking for the deeper truth in ourselves, and we can support this journey by looking for the same in others.

To illustrate, let's say that in the previous Zen story, every answer the first man gives to the Elder—that he would buy the sweetest hay, etc.—is a lie he told in order to win the position. End of story: He is out of consideration.

Or, we could sense that he is fearful of losing the opportunity to train with the Elder and is longing for a way to serve his community. The man's core emotions, which we can discover beneath the façade of the lie, are the real truth of the moment.

Belief 2: "It's Best to Take It Slow"

Our physical wounds take time to heal. A cut on our hand may need days or weeks to scab and scar. We have learned to be patient with our physical ailments and to live with woundedness. We have also, unfortunately, transposed this thinking onto our psychic wounds. All healing, we have come to believe, is best taken slow, or else we adjust poorly, and the efforts backfire. Yet Diogenes did not ruminate long before throwing away his bowl—he embraced change rapidly, on the spot. So can we.

By way of a modern example, let's consider smoking cessation. The average U.S. smoker makes more than three attempts at quitting smoking. Of the 24 percent of Americans who have successfully quit smoking, more than half attribute their success to willpower and quitting *cold turkey*—on the spot, on their own, with no supplemental medication or counseling. The contemporary tools of the gradual approach—the nicotine patches, nicotine gums, and electronic cigarettes—were, combined, responsible for just 8 percent of successful attempts at quitting. From the perspective of former smokers themselves, the immediate approach is, by far, the key to success.[4]

After discovering these findings, I then reviewed the major changes I had made in my life, which included quitting alcohol and becoming a vegetarian, and realized that I did every one of them … cold turkey.

The actual healing—the deep transformation that restores wellness—occurs in an instant. What often takes time is for our bodies, our feelings, and our thought and lifestyle patterns to align themselves with our inner Balance. It takes time to rebuild new neural connections, new patterns and ways of being. Remember, we are healing from the inside out. One of the biggest impediments to healing is simply being unaware that we are already healed.

We can sense that the healing has occurred in a number of ways. Sometimes our Dreamself is the messenger, and sometimes our conscious self is made aware through revelation of another sort. Virtually every time there is a change in feeling, a dynamic tension within that creates a certain disconnectedness with our status quo situation. This is our sign to become actively involved in the flowering of our healing.

The actual healing occurs in an instant, yet it must be encouraged. When we choose to wait to heal or resign ourselves to the gradual approach, we allow this spark to sputter out. I once thought the odds of kicking a habit would be in my favor if I just waited until everything was right—a supportive relationship, low stress, and a fulfilling activity to replace my habit. There was only one problem: It didn't work.

What's more, my resolve was by far the strongest when I was struggling the most with my addiction—when its fallout was being rubbed in my face and I was so disgusted with myself that I didn't see any hope. I had nothing more to lose and everything to gain. I could no longer fool myself into thinking that if only I waited until my life was on a smooth track, I'd be able to conquer my demon. I accepted that if I could start when I was at my lowest, I knew it could only get better.

Belief 3: "I'm Doing Fine"

Even if we've accepted that healing begins in the now, we may be thwarted by the sense that nothing *needs* to change since we're getting along just fine. We're content to float along undisturbed—and also unfulfilled. We are creatures of habit and pattern. Unfortunately, dysfunctional lifestyles and relationships become normal to us, and we adapt to sustain them. Yes, it may be that you are fine. It may be that nothing *needs* to change, though perhaps, deep down, you *want* change to happen.

We may also cling to a thought, belief, or lifestyle for fear of its opposite, which we put great effort into protecting ourselves from. The phenomenon is called *dichotomous thinking.* It is *either/or* and *all or nothing* thinking in which we ignore the possibility of ambiguity, duality, or the presence of gray between black and white. It keeps us from knowing the whole truth—and sometimes from discovering that the greater truth is what we resisted.

Let's take the example of people who have chosen to be poor. It may be for idealistic reasons or as a rebellion from their wealthy family heritage. They are typically as obsessed with money (to meet living expenses) as those who strive for material abundance. Those who adopt quiet, unassuming mannerisms in response to their violent, assertive upbringings often invite abusers into their lives, only to perpetuate the abuser-victim cycle. Those who work constantly to become independent and have free time have none when they become slaves to their dream. Meanwhile, those who overachieve to attract recognition and friends distance themselves from others by their overachievement.

Belief 4: "I Just Need to Open Up"

The *I'm doing fine* fallacy is indicative of another problem in our culture: We are loath to genuinely communicate our feelings. We hide behind neutral or token emotional statements. Our catharsis becomes reflexive and merely functional: We mime vulnerability to fulfill a social obligation to be expressive. In the process, we leave our true feelings undiscovered, unshared, and unexplored, which leaves us open yet opaque.

Openness is a layered action. It is not enough for us to simply open the door; we must also walk through it. Here are some tips on how:

1. **Allow yourself to experience your feelings fully.** Start by telling yourself that your feelings are yours and yours only. They are not about somebody else or a result of somebody else. What you want here is nothing except the raw stripped-down feeling. Scream it, write it, sing it, move with it—anything that helps you experience it fully and make it yours.

2. **Feel the pain.** Raw emotions have a physical component. Let it develop right along with the feeling. Maybe your chest tightens and your stomach burns. Maybe you clench your jaw or get a headache. It doesn't matter. Go there. For if you escape the pain, you escape the feeling.

3. **Keep it home.** The more intense the feeling and the associated pain, the more you're going to want to dump it on someone else. Here's the one time when *yeah-buts* are appropriate. When you catch yourself thinking, "I'm feeling so crabby because so-and-so …" say, "Yeah, but I chose to be in that relationship," or whatever the case might be.

4. **Let the feeling take its course.** You might end up feeling exhausted and flat, and maybe tired or shaky. I call it the cool-down phase. It's the same as how you feel after a run or other intense physical activity. Take care of yourself. Go for a walk, make some tea, grab a snack; whatever helps to make you feel relaxed, comfortable, and nurtured.

5. **Prepare to be amazed.** When your reactive feelings have burned off, your core feelings can now surface.

Belief 5: "I Am a Complex Emotional Being"

We can be straightforward in our emotional expression—if we choose to see ourselves that way. Instead, we often settle for what our culture tells us: that we are *complex*. We have come up with many terms to describe our emotional selves, and we have created so many definitions for those terms—all in our ceaseless attempt to express ourselves and be fundamentally understood. I've come to see such attempts as the rational mind gone awry. The more complex and verbose we get, the further away we drift from where we are trying to go.

By simplifying the language of our emotional expression, we can be candid *and* direct. If we were to go deep into our minds, into that ancient place of knowing, where we think without thought and express without words, we would find the four core emotions that drive our psycho-emotional expression and can serve as the basis of our revised vocabulary:

1. **Fear**: a lack of knowing. We fear only what we don't know: Either we don't know what's out there (as in fear of the dark) or we don't know how to handle it.

2. **Longing**: seeking relationship. When we feel longing, it fuels our continual and ever-present thirst for relationship; it is the glue that keeps us in relationship.

3. **Sadness**: an inability to give. We are here for one reason: to gift our beauty and uniqueness to those around us. Giving is receiving; neither can occur without the other, and we must give before we can receive since giving creates the space for receiving.

4. **Joy**: being in the now. It is the state of bliss we naturally find ourselves in when we are fully aware and attuned.

Every feeling that we have is either one of these core emotions or a spin-off. When I limit my vocabulary to these four terms, I am able to quickly recognize and express how I feel. I'm no longer fumbling for the *right* word when I'm not concerned with words—instead I'm focused on the core emotion that lies beneath verbal language.

Belief 6: "All We Need is Love"

You may be wondering, "Where is *love* on the list of core emotions?" When it comes to interrogating our feelings as part of our healing process, love is a bit of a red herring. It is a misnomer.

You seldom find the word *love* used in this book, since as an emotion, it does not exist. What we call *love* contains elements of all four of the core emotions: fear, longing, sadness, and joy. This is not to denigrate love or deny its existence. Rather, it is to understand that love is an experience and an action more than it is an emotion with clear contours that we can isolate.

Contemporary healing approaches focus too much on love and ignore the core emotions that inform it, each of which deserves examination. These approaches focus on the surface experience instead of dissecting it to work with the individual issues of fear, longing, sadness, and joy that are at the root of the struggle.

Instead of addressing issues of finding, rekindling, or fixing love, our healing would be better served if we asked what we really mean when we say *love*. You'll find that doing so leads you to employ the language of the four core emotions and, as a result, brings you closer to identifying the core issue or core motivations.

When a person says, "I need more love from you," what might he be saying? It could be that he is experiencing fear about the sincerity of your feelings; or, it may be that he is longing for a deeper sense of connection; or perhaps he is sad that he feels unable to give to you, so he also feels unable to receive; or it may be that he is joyful in the relationship and wants to expand that feeling. As you can see, relying on the word *love* alone leaves us unclear.

Like *love*, the term *hate* is a catch-all. And as with love, hate per se does not exist. Yet, there is clearly something going on. People quit talking to each other, move away, and even kill each other due to what they call hate. When I say, "I hate that person," what am I feeling? Recalling times when I hated, I had intense feelings of jealousy or anger. At other times, I felt judged or rejected. At still other times, I remember reacting to a bruised ego or feeling insecure. What I called hate could have been one clear emotion or a combination of emotions—most often fear and longing.

When we can expose hate for what it is—one or a combination of our core emotions—we can better take ownership of the feeling instead of externalizing, blaming, or projecting onto others. I remember one woman who said she absolutely hated the man she was with for three years. She had a child with this man, and she felt totally dominated by his passion and idealism. After she was able to own her feelings—and it took her going through the process several times to do so—she realized that she was really frustrated with herself for not being able to actualize her dreams, and as a result, she was externalizing onto her partner. She went to him and told him how much she admired him for the example he was providing and that she realized she had father issues that she was projecting onto him. She then thanked him for being the catalyst that brought them up so she could work on them.

Belief 7: "I Can Heal While I'm Using"

We can't heal through an addiction when we are *using*, that is, when we are under the influence of our numbing, soothing "fix." In fact, the opposite happens: We strengthen our addiction. We need to be free of it in order to see our demon unclothed and have the uncluttered clarity and energy to face it. Anything less is just self-enabling.

Albert Einstein noted that you can't solve a problem from the level at which it was created; you must seek a new and higher level of order and alignment.[5] This statement echoes the traditional wisdom that *What we feed, grows*. When we are hopelessly immersed in our behaviors, we may have to step outside them, outside the environment that fosters them, to gain perspective and the wherewithal to approach their healing.

Belief 8: "Stress and Drama Are Bad"

People who live close to the means and ends of their existence, such as hunter-gatherers, experience a lot of stress in their lives, yet they are generally happy people. So what makes stress beneficial to them and not to most of us?

The primary difference is that the stress they experience is largely short-term, such as on the hunt. There is a build-up of tension and a flurry of activity, followed by a period of rest before the next hunt.

Our stress, on the other hand, is typically long-term, which makes it debilitating. Whether it be a dead-end job, financial problems, or relationship issues, the associated stress is usually chronic and difficult to resolve. Stress itself is not the problem, as we need stress to stimulate hormonal flow and sharpen our senses. To eliminate it would cause us to lead hollow, humdrum existences. Instead, we work to reduce our experience of *chronic* stress while also seeking ways to bring short-term stress into our lives—for instance, adventure sports or tension-building movies.

We evolved in an environment where, in addition to short-term stress, we also experienced drama—the drama of the hunt, weather changes, and unforeseen crises of all sorts. Drama is the dynamic tension created by an unfolding scene. We evolved the skills to deal with these dramas and to derive positive reinforcement from handling them effectively.

When drama escalates, our adrenal gland releases hormones that energize us, causing us to feel super-sensitized, keenly alert, and fully present. We ride an emotional high, regardless of whether the outcome is positive or negative. It is this high that we crave and sometimes become addicted to, especially if we do not have naturally occurring drama in our lives. When we lead drama-enriched lives, our drama hunger is satisfied, and we run no risk of addiction to drama high.

In our present culture, our needs are provided for us, and we're protected from virtually all of the challenges that were part and parcel of our hunter-gatherer ancestors' lives. This presents us with a dilemma. We are designed for drama, yet we are exposed only to the cheap drama of civilized culture—pettiness, gossip, celebrity, etc.—and not the grander drama of being directly connected to the means and ends of our existence.

Other patterns I've seen people enact are withholding information, not answering questions directly, and challenging people's positions to create drama-producing dynamics. Sexual and relationship tension, including many practices in the BDSM (bondage, domination, sadism, masochism) community, are also designed to create drama.

On a grander scale, international competition, whether it be economic or military, creates drama in our lives. And let's not forget the drama that is intrinsic to many religious practices.

As with stress, we don't want to eliminate drama from our lives—instead, we want to acknowledge our human need to experience it and, in doing so, begin to access it in ways that nurture healthy relationships.

Belief 9: "My Ego Is My Nemesis"

Many of us hold the belief that the ego is bad. We have heard so much about how being stuck in our egos keeps us from being present and empathetic—or how it creates defensiveness and distance, which makes us reactive and oftentimes aggressive.

All of this is true. Yet, this is just what the ego is designed to do, and in certain circumstances, we can be thankful for it. The ego steps to the forefront when our fight/flight mechanism is triggered. The catch is that we evolved in a natural environment where there were real threats to our survival. There were weather extremes and the dangers of the hunt, and there were times where we were the hunted. Here it was essential that the ego take over, create boundaries, and have us assume a defensive/aggressive position.

In our day, the ego is alive and well, yet the threats to our well-being are more perceived than real. We create our realities much more so than did our hunter-gatherer ancestors. For most of us, the biggest risk of the hunt is coming home late with the groceries. Instead, the threats to our existence, at least the *perceived* threats to our existence, are largely psycho-emotional.

When someone is being stalked by a tiger, it is no perceived reality, and the ego best commands the situation quickly and efficiently, as that state of reality is absolute. The trick in our current culture is to work with our egos rather than letting them control us by default.

YOU ARE ALWAYS YOURSELF

One common way we work against our egos is by saying things like, "I'm different with different people." The reality is that on a deeper level, it does not matter whom I am engaged with at any particular moment, I'm enacting the very same thing that I enact in any other relationship. I am working with my core self, core nature, and core emotions. My ego is one facet of how I express these—it is not my excuse to lose perspective of them. It has nothing to do with my relationship with that person or this person—it has to do with me and who I am and how I am.

Belief 10: "I Need to Trust in You."

We also work against our ego when it comes to trust. Often when we have our trust broken, we react from the perspective of our ego, which wants to protect us, and we tell ourselves to be more careful—less gullible—next time. Yet, there is an element of truth to our ego's voice that would serve us well to hear: Trust should be informed, not blind, and it should be contextual.

Some of us extend trust without giving adequate consideration to the potential consequences. Trust itself is not the problem—it is a beautiful aspect of the human experience. Perhaps the greatest, most rewarding moments of trust are those in which there is great uncertainty as well. Nevertheless, we place ourselves at risk when we project trust onto other people, circumstances, or relationships without knowing whether it is appropriate or deserved in that moment.

Imagine that my five-year-old child is playing in the yard and her ball rolls out onto the street. Am I wise in trusting her to remember at that moment that I told her not to run out into the street? Might I be wiser to trust in the fact that a five-year-old's life is all about the now? And the now for her is retrieving the ball she had been enjoying.

Or, let's say you are seeing somebody who is not feeling fulfilled in the relationship: Is it wise to trust in that person's fidelity, or is it reasonable to trust in the possibility that she wants to seek fulfillment elsewhere? When we choose the latter, we ground our trust in knowing, and we avoid a scenario where we end up saying "I trusted you; how could you do that to me?" Instead, you can talk with her about the realities of your relationship and help to assure that everyone's needs are being met, thus helping to arrive at a different outcome. The answer, then, is not about *not* trusting; rather, it is about knowing where to place our trust.

Chapter in a Page

Personal responsibility in our healing begins by courageously examining our preconceived beliefs. This requires beginner's mind—open, nonjudgmental, ready to receive. Unburdened by false ideas, we unleash our potential.

A new look at old beliefs:

- We can reshape the past. We embrace our past by learning its lessons without feeling victimized. Changing how we perceive our past changes our present.

- Transformative healing occurs instantaneously. What takes time is for our bodies, feelings, thoughts, and lifestyles to align with our inner Balance.

- We are creatures of habit and pattern. We easily adapt to dysfunctional lifestyles and relationships. Being content to float along undisturbed does not indicate we are living a fulfilling life.

- Attempting to communicate our feelings can become reflexive and merely functional: We mime vulnerability to fulfill a social

obligation to be expressive. In the process, we leave our true
feelings unexplored, which leaves us open yet opaque.

- Our emotional world can be expressed simply. Only four core
  emotions drive us: fear (a lack of knowing), longing (a desire for
  relationship), sadness (an inability to give), and joy (a state of
  bliss when we are fully in the now). Every feeling we have is one
  of these core emotions or a spin-off.

- Love is not one of the four core emotions but can contain elements of each. Our cultural obsession with *love* keeps us at the
  surface level of understanding rather than examining what is
  beneath our experience of love.

- When immersed in dysfunctional behaviors and addictions, we
  must quit them *cold turkey* to gain perspective. We need to be
  free of them in order to have the clarity to face them. Einstein
  noted that you can't solve a problem from the level at which it
  was created.

- Stress and drama sharpen awareness for those who live close to
  the means and ends of their existence. By acknowledging our
  human need to experience stress and drama, we can access them
  in ways that nurture healthy relationships.

- The ego is designed to create defensiveness and distance useful
  to humans when their fight/flight mechanism is triggered, and
  annihilating ego misunderstands how adversity shaped human
  evolution. In contemporary society, threats to our well-being
  are more perceived than real. We can work with our egos rather
  than letting them control us or rejecting them.

- Trust should be informed and contextual. We place ourselves
  at risk when we project trust onto other people, circumstances,
  or relationships without knowing whether it is appropriate or
  deserved.

3: We Hang on to Old Beliefs Endnotes

1   Thomas McEvilley, *The Shape of Ancient Thought: Comparative Studies in Greek and Indian Philosophies* (Skyhorse Publishing, Inc., 2012), 232.

2   Koko Willis and Pali Jae Lee, *Tales from the Night Rainbow*, 15.

3   Oberpfälzische Blätter für Sonn (Böes, 1877), 27.

4   Frank Newport, "Most US Smokers Want to Quit, Have Tried Multiple Times," *Gallup*, last modified 31 July 2013, accessed 14 October 2020, http://www.gallup.com/poll/163763/smokers-quit-tried-multiple-times.aspx.

5   "Atomic Education Urged by Einstein," *New York Times* (New York), May 25, 1946, 11.

4: We Resort to Boundaries

One brisk, spring morning as you stroll through the woods, you stumble across a small pond. From a distance its surface, flat and smooth like a mirror, glistens in the sunlight. A leaf rests poised on it. The Renaissance artist and scientist Leonardo Da Vinci once posed the question of what exactly divides the sea from the sky—is the boundary the air or the water?[1] As you ponder this question, you stoop along the shore. With ease you pass your hand through the water's surface. You gather a handful of pebbles to skip, then watch as they skid along the surface before passing irrevocably beneath it. Many months later, in the quiet of a winter morning, you return to the pond and marvel that you can walk across its frozen surface. The answer to Da Vinci's question, you decide, lies in the winter: The boundary between sea and sky is the ice. Even so, you wonder, what is the boundary between the sea and the ice, or the ice and the sky?

Boundaries are *bona fide*, in both senses of the term: the contemporary, meaning *real*, and the original from the era of Da Vinci, meaning *in good faith*.[2] The realness of boundaries is a product of the faith we place in them—and just as faith is inherently marked by an element of doubt, boundaries too are open-ended. This is not to say that boundaries do not exist. They do—however, just like the surface of the pond, they are less fixed than we might like to believe. It may be more appropriate, in fact, to call them thresholds. As the story of the pond shows, boundaries divide, and they grant entry; they repel the leaf and embrace the stone; they transform, and they may also disappear—consider how, in a drought, the pond may evaporate entirely.

Part of why boundaries are so fluid is their dependence on context—something we often ignore when speaking of boundaries in our culture. Take the concept of *building a wall* between ourselves and another person: It appears to be a clear-cut boundary—the wall, we think, speaks for itself. Yet there are many different kinds of walls. There are walls designed to limit mobility or to block vision; they may be used to divide, support, or protect a space; they may be used to keep others out or to keep them in.[3] Each wall has a distinct function and a particular context. The word *wall*, like the word *boundary*, helps us visualize it, yet this only gets us so far.

There are also personal and interpersonal boundaries, which may be physical or even mental and spiritual. The latter are much trickier and triggering. In the following pages, we discuss where boundaries help us and where they harm us. We honor the need to recognize personal boundaries, remaining attentive to how we can prevent them from becoming barriers to our healing. We explore what it means to live a life beyond our current understanding of boundaries.

Just as we are willing to examine our old beliefs about healing, it is important for us to be open to challenging our preconceived notions about boundaries. The way we think about them can make a significant difference in our healing. Consider this: If I have been given half a bowl of soup, do I complain that it is half empty or do I feel grateful that it is half full? Depending on how I perceive the boundary, and on which side of it I fall, makes the difference in whether I feel a sense of anger or joy.

Where Boundaries Help and Where They Hurt

Before exploring the pitfalls of the *boundaries approach* to emotional healing, I'd like to express its importance. In the short run, boundaries can help by creating a safe space for someone who does not have the tools to recognize dysfunctional relationship patterns and navigate his/her way around them. In many cases, boundaries are not only helpful, they are essential for an individual's immediate safety. Those who are abused and exploited or who carry the wound-edness of being abused and have not been able to develop adequate relationship skills benefit from boundaries.

Learning how to say "No" and how to establish and communicate personal boundaries is an important aspect of personal development in our culture, especially for survivors of abuse. At times, boundaries are necessary for our safety, security, and well-being.

Boundaries can also allow us to hide from a problem, evade shar-ing our truth, or avoid healing a relationship. In those cases, our boundary becomes about denial rather than self-preservation. We establish these false boundaries when we are avoiding some aspect of ourselves that either we, our society, or our religion deems to be undesirable, whether it's considered distasteful, illegal, immoral, or sinful. One way to tell if a boundary may be limiting is if it starts to take the form of externalizations, judgments, and criticisms.

Boundaries are a tool, not a belief system. Suppose I'm walking east to visit the pond mentioned previously, then I'm not walking west. I don't have to put up a boundary concerning walking west. It's just not where I'm going. It's not a part of my consciousness. It's not where I'm growing. However, if someone I encounter along the way begins to push me to go west, then I have to put up some resistance; I put up a boundary. Carrying that boundary with me from the get-go does not serve me, though.

Here's a more extended illustration. Let's say I'm struggling with alcohol. I just can't get on top of my addiction. Every time I'm around my friends and they want to go out for a beer, I'm out for the whole night and I get drunk and I can't make it to work the next morning. Eventually I realize I have to set up a boundary: no alcohol, not even one drink, since I have no control.

Now, after some time, if I get to a point where I realize I *don't* have to get drunk in order to have a good time with my friends, I can go out with them and enjoy a beer or two with self-control. I'm home on time to take care of myself, get to bed, and arrive early for work the next morning—then the following night, when my friends want to go out again, I can decline the invitation with ease. The drinking does not control me, and I no longer want it to.

BOUNDARIES AND BEING CENTERED

You may be wondering: "Is a person who has boundaries *un-centered?*" The answer is yes, when those boundaries are a product of fear, denial, or judgment rather than self-preservation or mindful awareness. In a moment of crisis, a boundary may be the very thing that keeps us calm and centered; it can also be the thing that allows us to avoid addressing our core emotions and returning to center.

As a point of clarity, just as we are all healed, we are all centered and self-aware. That is who we are, and that is our genetic heritage. Centeredness and self-awareness are also different for each person: There is no one gold standard we are trying to achieve. Someone might seem more or less centered or self-aware only in comparison to others.

So what happens if I keep the boundary? I continue to define myself as a victim—as a person dependent on that boundary to keep him away from excessive drinking—instead of a centered person, who no longer needs that boundary as he no longer desires to excessively drink. When I let go of the boundary, I can begin to more fully embrace my empowered self.

To describe boundaries as entirely *good* or *bad* is beside the point. What matters is that we engage in making and deconstructing boundaries with mindful awareness. We are each at different points in our personal healing journeys, and some of us may have a greater need for boundaries than others. That is okay. We cannot ask someone to give up what they don't yet have: Before we can begin to live an empowered life beyond boundaries, we first need to experience what it means to live an empowered life *with* boundaries—the ways they can protect, serve, and nurture us—which happens when we use them as tools, not principles.

Why Boundaries?

We evolved in a culture of abundance, where food, clothing, and shelter were ours for the taking or making. Our ancestors had a circle of support in their clan, where they had trusting, loving relationships with those they worked and played with. Those people were their siblings, cousins, uncles, aunts, parents, and grandparents. In such a culture of caring and plenty, self-protective boundaries were seldom needed. And when our ancestors did have unmet needs or threats to their well-being, they would typically have options other than boundaries, such as people from other clans, new habitat, or other skill sets, to turn to.

If this is our heritage, then why do we feel so secure with boundaries? This is the result of growing up in a culture of scarcity. Somebody other than us owns the commodities for meeting our food, clothing, and shelter needs, and somebody else controls their distribution. So we have to buy into their system in order to provide for ourselves and our families. And we have to compete with others in order to do so—and when we are in competition with each other, we are no longer in loving relationship with each other.

We have become accustomed to boundaries in our daily lives, from national borders to backyard fences, from speed limits to laws and alarm clocks. We have religious, political, and class boundaries. It only follows that we would set up boundaries in our personal lives as well, to protect us in our familial, intimate, and outside relationships.

These boundaries can leave us feeling isolated and condition us to be self-protective. As a result, few of us can truly say that we feel secure and happy. Instead, most of us can admit to feeling anxious and having unfulfilled longings. That makes us ripe for codependent relationships and being victimized in those relationships. Living in worry and isolation, we need defensive-protective mechanisms to feel safe. Boundaries not only fit the bill, they often end up being all we have to turn to.

In comparison, the un-boundaried approach to life and relationship—un-boundaried in the sense of casting aside false boundaries that perpetuate our denial, evasion, and fear—is conscious and engaged. We are centered and self-knowing enough to make relationship decisions and take care of crises and conflicts as they arise. This doesn't mean that I no longer turn to boundaries for help. We create temporary special-purpose boundaries that apply to the situation at hand (as with the previous alcohol story). Once the boundary has served its purpose, we let it go.

This approach comes from the Zen tradition and is a natural outpouring of the beginner's mind. In it, we say, "I used a boundary yesterday when I wasn't acting very centered—I couldn't figure out what might be best for me or the person I was with in the moment. However, today is a new day, and I am a new person. Let's see what it brings." You experience the boundaries, you leave them behind, then you use them—or not—as you choose.

Think of boundaries as a life raft. Your ship has sunk, and as long as you're out to sea, you want to stick with that life raft. Trying to swim to land without it is foolhardy. You would only be courting your own demise. And so we stay poised afloat the raft, on the border between sea and sky, between life and death, and know we are secure. There comes a point, though, when another ship arrives or the waves carry us to shore. When we step on land again, we can let go of the raft.

Boundaries and Relationship

Our relationships should be based on just that—relationship, not boundaries. That doesn't mean there are no boundaries in relationship.

It means that relationship requires communication, and as with all relationships, the closer we get and the fewer boundaries between us, the easier it is to communicate. We may rely on boundaries to structure how and what we communicate early on. Yet, over time, we use our communication to remove those boundaries that are based on fear or denial.

Allowing boundaries to become the modus operandi of a functioning relationship allows the relationship to become stagnant—this can apply to a relationship with ourselves, with other people, or even with non-human things. Let's consider the relationship between our species and gravity. We could have settled for the boundary presented to us initially by gravity: What goes up must come down. Instead, we pushed that boundary, though at times gravity pushed back; we fell, we got back up, and we continued pushing. We discovered the deeper properties of gravity and, as a result, we learned to fly. When we settle for the boundary, we deny ourselves the possibilities.

The concept of boundaries is rooted in ego perspective: I need to see myself as a distinct and autonomous entity in order to create a barrier between myself and others. This approach not only makes sense to those of us who come from an ego-based culture and are immersed in ego-based relationships, it also works—when in Rome, do as the Romans. However, it is a two-way street—along with the boundaries approach working, it reinforces the ego-based approach to relationship. When we use boundaries to guide us in relationship, we pair up with people who are similar to us. The same religion, the same values, the same ethnicity, and the same interests. I call these *compatible* relationships since they are safe and comfortable, though oftentimes they are not very stimulating. That is due to the fact that, to a large degree, we have chosen a mirror image of ourselves. The person reinforces who I already am, without having much new to offer. So we stay in familiar territory, seldom venturing out into our frontier.

Complementary relationships, on the other hand, are born in the frontier. When we step out from behind our boundaries, we step out onto the frontier where everything is new and anything is possible. It is there that we meet other people out on their frontiers. Rather than being threatened by differences, by people with different backgrounds, perspectives, and ways of doing things, we burn with a thirst to hear their stories and learn from them. We are stimulated and inspired by change and new direction. Although once we would feel overwhelmed and vulnerable in such a situation, we now not only feel right at home, we wouldn't have it any other way. *The only constant is change* becomes our motto, whereas in the days of our boundaried existence, our motto had to be *Change is dangerous.*

Boundaries and Fear

At the core, boundary thinking is related to our core emotion of fear—fear of losing control, fear of self, and fear of others. We fear what we don't know or don't understand, and to employ a boundary tends to paralyze us in our fear. A boundary can become a crutch. We learn to rely upon it to walk, and we forget that we would typically walk without it.

When we embrace our fear and allow it to guide us, we grow into our innate capacity the same way as a child who is learning to walk ventures forth a few more steps each day, each a little faster and more self-assured than the day before. With the *embrace-your-fear approach*, which I also call the *engaged approach*, we replace structure and protectivism with consciousness and empowerment.

However, most of us never get there on our own, due to our culture's continual reinforcement of the boundaries approach. We have laws and regulations, beliefs and social conventions, all of which impose boundaries on our behaviors. These crutches not only get us by without having to be directly engaged, they also become an addictive drug that we cannot get by without. What comes to mind when you envision a lawless state or people without beliefs and morals? Yes, a boundary-based life has become our norm, yet it is hardly normal. Our ancestors lived for millennia in an environment where mores were considered more a personal responsibility than an enforceable directive.

When we become accustomed to relying upon boundaries, we divert our focus from the deep healing we need in order to make lasting change in our lives. To illustrate: I'm walking down a trail and I come to a drop-off. Immediately I'm gripped with fear—my life would be imperiled if I continued. So I set up a boundary: I refuse to go near that drop-off. That's all well and fine, as I have taken care of myself in the moment.

However, since I dwell in boundary consciousness, odds are I plan to only go so far down that trail in the future so I don't come near the drop-off. And there is a good chance that I also plan to avoid other trails that might have drop-offs. I rely upon the boundary to protect me, to the degree that I start planning my outdoor experiences around it. On the other hand, if I were to embrace my fear when I came upon the drop-off, it would become a part of my consciousness, there to guide me to finding a safe route to the valley below and whatever lies beyond.

In that way, boundaries can serve us in the moment, while they backfire as well. Consider the legend of the meeting of the wild animals told by the Tsimshian Indians of Alaska. In it, Grizzly Bear gathers together all the large and small animals, even the insects, to address the threat of the Tsimshian hunters. The hunters are talented, and the animals are afraid. Grizzly Bear proposes the creation of a new, impassable boundary—the coldest winters the earth has ever seen, so cold that the human hunters can no longer hunt. The large animals heartily agree, though after much silence Porcupine responds. She says the large animals, with their warm fur, would survive such a winter; the insects and small animals would die. She also tells her Relations that this new, coldest of all winters is sure to destroy the roots and plants that feed the larger animals, which would cause them to starve. Grizzly Bear and the other creatures agree with Porcupine's wisdom, and they leave the seasons unchanged.[4]

Boundaries and Healing

This chapter began with the question of what divides the sea from the sky, though many of you may be wondering: "What is it that divides my unhealed self from my healed self?" The answer is: thinking that there is an unhealed self separate from your healed self. When we think we are divided, we create the boundary that divides us. Remember, we are already centered, whole, and healed in our core self. We may have dysfunctional behavior or relationship patterns, yet that does not mean that we ourselves are intrinsically dysfunctional.

Some of us may say to ourselves that until we are *perfectly* whole, until we have no faults or cracks or boundaries, we are broken— though this does not help us either. Wholeness includes those moments when we put up a boundary for our self-preservation; when we say "No" and mean it; when we are out at sea and cling to the raft. Neither is wholeness perfection—*wholeness* includes the *hole*. There are moments on our healing journey when we stumble, react from fear, and put up a boundary—that doesn't mean we have failed. Remember, what matters is that we are aware of where we put up boundaries and also of our ability to take them down.

Chapter in a Page

Boundaries exist, and they are adaptable. Boundaries can be personal and interpersonal; they may be physical or even mental and spiritual. Just as we examined beliefs about healing, we must challenge our preconceived notions about boundaries.

In the short run, boundaries help create a safe space for some-one without the tools or wherewithal to recognize dysfunctional relationship patterns and navigate around them. Sometimes boundaries are essential for an individual's immediate safety.

Otherwise, boundaries let us hide from a problem, evade sharing our truth, or avoid healing a relationship. These boundaries are about denial, not self-preservation. We establish false boundaries when we refuse to deal with some aspect of ourselves. Boundaries that limit us involve externalizations, judgments, and criticisms. Remember, boundaries are a tool, not a belief system.

Boundary thinking stems from our core emotion of fear—fear of losing control, fear of self, and fear of others. We fear the unknown, and boundaries tend to paralyze us in our fear. When a boundary is unrelated to self-preservation, it becomes a crutch. We forget we can walk without it.

Think of boundaries as a life raft. Your ship has sunk, but eventually another ship arrives or the waves carry you to shore. When you step on land again, you can let go of the raft. This Zen approach harnesses beginner's mind. It guides us to approach each day anew, making the best decisions for the moment at hand. You experience the boundaries, you leave them behind, then you use them—or not—as you choose.

There is no division between your unhealed self and your healed self. When we think we are divided, we create the boundary that divides us. We are already centered, whole, and healed in our core self.

4: We Resort to Boundaries Endnotes

1   Leonardo da Vinci, ed. E. MacCurdy, *The Notebooks* (London: Reynal & Hitchock, 1938).

2   "Definition of Bona Fide in English:," *Lexico*, last modified 2020, accessed 14 October 2020, https://www.lexico.com/en/definition/bona_fide.

3   Wendy Brown, *Walled States, Waning Sovereignty* (New York: Zone, 2010), 25.

4   Richard Erdoes and Alfonso Ortiz, "The Meeting of the Wild Animals," *American Indian Myths and Legends*, 413-15.

5: We Give Ourselves More Choices

We approach our lives either from the *head*—the rational, analytical, dichotomous mind—or from the *heart*—a place of deep centeredness, where our limbic mind, senses, emotions, instincts, ancestral memories, and intellect all come together in council to guide us. This approach is the mark of a life in deep attunement with ourselves and the world, as it is much deeper and older than our rational mind. This doesn't mean the rational mind is a burden to us. Quite the contrary, it is an integral part of who we are—it is just not our core self.

The Illusion of Choice

We feel centered within ourselves, content, and clear when we come from our hearts. We do not have to choose to live and act from the heart—it is our natural inclination. Fear is most often the reason our ego takes over and we resort to our rational minds. The ego controls us through rationale. And rightfully so, as stress, depression, lack of acknowledgment, insecurity, power struggles, and unfulfilledness are all shades of fear. We aim to ameliorate fear, as it un-centers us and leaves us physically and emotionally debilitated. The purpose of the rational mind is to work through what un-centers us and guide us back to the heart.

To help visualize this dynamic, let's return to the bowl of soup from the previous chapter. If I see my bowl as half full, I am coming from my Heart-of-Hearts: I have food, I am grateful for it, and I have room for more. If I see my bowl as half empty, I am coming from a place of fear: I worry about running out, I grow anxious, and I have to focus on getting my bowl filled. The drive comes from the innate need to escape the debilitating effects of chronic fear. The rational mind is the source of this drive. It tells us, very reasonably, that we need more money, a bigger house, a better job, a more beautiful partner, etc., in order to be safe, secure, and whole.

Our culture has provided an alluring name for this drive: freedom of choice. Isn't this one of the premises upon which our Western way of life is based? We sincerely believe that we thrive on options, whether they be political, religious, or culinary. When we don't have them, "Give me the freedom to choose" becomes our battle cry. Our dichotomous mind then concludes that without this freedom, we can only be left with totalitarianism.

Yet, when we come from our heart, there is no choice. Our Lifepath is given, and the *Beauty Way,* which is dwelling in the bliss of the moment, with little regret for the past or care for the future, lies before us. This is not to deny our human ability to discern, analyze, and act on those analyses; nor does it mean that the Beauty Way represses us. The Beauty Way does not take away a *right*; it removes a redundancy. When we come from the heart, we have no need for "freedom of choice," since we see the truth beyond the rhetoric: We have needs, and we must meet those needs. There is no choice. (In fact, 95-99 percent of our "choices" are made subconsciously, in our limbic process.[1] The 1-5 percent that we make consciously are more often rationalizations to support clarities that we already have.)

The rational mind splinters the truth of the moment, then fabricates "choices" out of the splinters. Consider, in reference to our bowl of soup: Do I wait to eat? Do I add salt? Do I eat with a spoon? What size spoon? Choices *ad infinitum.* From the perspective of the heart, however, it doesn't matter whether the bowl is half empty or half full, and it doesn't matter how I eat or what condiments I use. From the perspective of the heart, I have a need—hunger—and I must meet that need—by eating. If I want to remain centered, there is no choice. If I want to live according to my rational mind, then yes, there are "choices." Ultimately, the question of whether the bowl is half empty or half full is an illusion. The longer I spend deliberating over it, the longer I am distracted from my underlying need.

The decision to live according to the heart does not mean we are acting *irrationally*. The rational mind and the limbic mind, you'll remember, are not in competition. To live according to the heart does not mean that we are denying our rational mind. It means that we are using our rational mind to serve the limbic mind rather than the other way around. The rational mind, and the choices that it manifests, are meant to steer us back toward centeredness—that place where we are clear in our motivations, in tune with our surroundings, and in the best state to meet our needs. In fact, you might even say that that is the most rational place to be.

Often, the ego complicates the matter. Let's consider the need to express our Truth. From the perspective of the heart, there is no choice: We have a need which we must meet. Yet from the perspective of the ego, there are many choices: what words to use, whom to tell, when to tell it, or whether to express it at all. Rather than choices, they are again merely illusions. If I am angry, I can *choose* not to voice it, or I can carefully *choose* which words to use or not use. Yet my Truth is written on my face, heard in my tone of voice, and expressed in my body language. No matter what supposed choices I make, the bottom line is that I am expressing my Truth.

Like *freedom of choice*, the concept of *free will* is a function of our rational mind and does not exist from the perspective of the heart. This does not mean that the way of the heart is one of enslavement or tyranny. Nor does it mean that we cannot act or exert influence in our lives. It means that from the perspective of the heart, there is only one way to act: in the way that meets our needs. I cannot will away my needs—my need to breathe air, drink water, or share my Truth, for instance. Instead, I am free to meet those needs.

What We Left Behind

Imagine for a moment that we are not born with free will and that our choices amount to no more than changing costumes. By most people's definition of what makes us human, we have just stepped down the evolutionary ladder and become animals. Although, what evidence do we have that we are any different than a Wolf—beyond the simple fact that we are of a different species? Every human once lived like Wolves—hunting, gathering, running, and living and dying within our respective clans. Like Wolves, we lived lives composed of needs, the imperative to meet them, and the capacity to do so. We still do.

What's more, consider the words of Vernon Harper, of the Northern Cree in Canada: "Some people say that animals are ignorant, but in many ways they're really smarter than us. You don't see a dog trying to be an eagle. You don't see a squirrel trying to be a wolf. The same with the plants … all of the plants have been given specific instructions from the Creator on what to do. Plants and animals follow their instructions. It's the human beings who don't follow theirs."[2]

The pack was the life of a Wolf, the clan was the life of a Human; we shared similar instructions. In the pack and the clan lay comfort, caring, and a sense of purpose. The clan and the pack came first, for without them there was barely the chance of survival, much less use of life, and a weakened sense of belonging. It is only very recently in our species' history that we did anything otherwise—that we began to stop following our instructions.

With the breakdown of the role of the clan in our culture, the individual became predominant. Preferences and prejudices turned into life pursuits. Peace with each other in balance with nature—or some semblance thereof—needed to be legislated and moralized. Even as we live the effects of this shift in our culture—the dysfunctional relationships, depression, anxiety, chronic stress and fear, to name a few—we still cling to the battle cries of *free will* and *freedom of choice.*

These concepts have become sacred cows. So sacred that we allow them to inhibit our healing. I am reminded of the words of a Polar Eskimo, who said: "It is generally believed that white men have quite the same minds as small children. They are easily angered, and when they cannot get their will they are moody and, like children, have the strangest ideas and fancies."[3] We are at this moment a culture of angry individuals living in a world of fancy—out of balance, un-centered, out of tune with who we were and who we are—and bowing down before it.

We have become like the Wolves who, long ago, abandoned the pack and became Dogs, in the process losing much of their sleekness and cunning. Tugging at chains and leashes, they cried, "Give me the freedom to choose," and they were given sticks to chase instead of Deer. To the clan, you and I are vitally important. We are each uniquely contributing organs within a living organism. At the same time, we are expendable—organs sacrificed for the well-being of the organism. A hand can survive quite well without a finger, not the other way around.

CHOICES AND OUR CORE NATURE

The illusion of choices becomes clear when we revisit what we have already discussed about our core nature. You recall that our core nature is composed of our archetypal energy, our genetically based character trait as a stay-at-homer or trailblazer, and our gender role. They are things we do not choose, although others may try to assign them to us (especially our gender role).

To be told that we can or should *choose* our archetypal energy places us at risk of misidentifying ourselves and then working against our core nature. Our rational mind has the capacity to analyze our energy patterns, and it may tempt us to choose our archetype. If we live from the heart, though, there is no choice—we simply live, and in doing so we live out our archetypal energy, our character trait, and our gender role. The Truth of who we are is something that transcends the concept of choice.

Choices Can Be Suicide

We evolved in an environment where we ate what the hunters and foragers brought home, we moved with the seasons and the game animals, we listened to our dreams, and we had the enrichment and lifelong security of a close-knit clan. Now we are bombarded with the illusion of choices: which restaurant, school, occupation, counselor, vacation destination, person to date, place to live. Does it really matter whether I choose a silver or blue car, a cheap or expensive car? I am still driving a car. Does it really matter where I eat or which apartment I choose to rent? I am still not connected to the clan life that is my heritage or to the source of my food, and I am still lonely.

In terms of our healing, one reason we are emotionally sick is precisely a result of too many choices. We have become, in the words of clinical psychologist Randi Gunther, "obsessive-compulsive" with making choices.[4] There is such a thing as too many choices. When we are faced with a high volume of them, we are more likely to experience regret, self-blame, a sense of missed opportunity, and unmet expectations.[5, 6]

There is also the case that when faced with more choices, we find ourselves unable to make *any* choice at all. The hallmark of our civilized freedom is, it seems, the thing that actually tyrannizes us. In fact, experiments ranging from buying jam to writing essays, from retirement plan contributions to speed dating, show us that having *fewer* choices leads to higher satisfaction.[7, 8, 9]

Yes, the option to pick a word with twenty synonyms or indulge in one of thirty-two flavors of ice cream gives comfort of a sort, yet is it the deep, soul-satisfying enjoyment that comes from using our skills to provide for our people? The freedom of choice we are designed for is not whether we have ice cream or cheesecake for dessert; rather, it's how we can serve our people, our clan. It is the way of life that is rooted to our limbic mind, our heart, not the rational mind. It is *choice*, yet not as we know it and use the term. In its purest sense, the freedom of choice I am speaking of is the conscious steps we take to foster our maturation and evolve our talents, so we can better care for ourselves and serve our people.

Using Food to Reconnect

My references to food demonstrate where we let our *freedom of choice* run amuck, as well as where we can most clearly return to centeredness. Food helped me understand the illusion of freedom of choice.

I grew up in Wisconsin in the 1950s in a small town of subsistence dairy farmers. I spent a lot of time on my friends' farms and shared many meals with them. Over time it became clear to me that the more things and choices we have, the more confused we become, while a peasant family with just two or three nourishing foods is happy. I wasn't the only one to notice: The United Nations' 2015 World Happiness Report specifies family, friendships, trust, and empathy as some of the strongest indicators of well-being at the level of the individual and the nation; note that freedom of choice and having *more* choices are not mentioned in that list.[10] If what we desire is happiness and to walk the Beauty Way, we may need to reconsider our cultural battle cries.

I remember eating at my grandparents' farm sixty years ago. They raised twelve children on thirty-nine hardscrabble acres. The food was down-home, wholesome fare, though not the variety I was accustomed to. And it changed from one visit to the next, depending on the season. Yet from what I saw, there was always enough to pass around the great round-oak dining room table a couple of times. And it tasted so good after a hard day in the field—especially after watching my rosy-cheeked grandma pull pan after pan out of the woodstove oven with those stained potholders that told of the many meals they helped serve. We all ate heartily, enjoying the meal and each other's company. There were no issues around the food and no deliberations about choices; there was only gratefulness and camaraderie.

Groups come together and break up around food, and between the two extremes, there can be endless discussions seeking some resolution around the topic. Sometimes I get involved, and at other times I sit back and listen. Listening with my heart rather than my head allows me to hear what people are saying beneath their defensiveness and rationalizations. Their impassioned statements show

how real their world of endless variety and abundance, of beliefs and causes, is to them.

While I listen, a memory sometimes comes back of me paddling into a beaver pond and a hundred Ducks exploding out of the sedges in front of me. One stayed behind, floating lifeless on the surface. I gave thanks to the Duck People for remembering my hunger, and I feasted. Another day on the same wilderness stream, the Trout People gifted me similarly, and another day it was the Muskrat People. I didn't think about politics or preferences, I didn't fret about choices: I only gave thanks and ate.

When we give ourselves more choices, we lose perspective. We forget that we are already walking the Beauty Way. We get so caught up in the possibilities our rational mind has dutifully distinguished that we forget what our core needs are. When we cannot identify our core needs, we are no longer living a life that is centered. Thankfully, we can return to balance and find our way again. To do that, we stop dwelling in choices and start dwelling in the heart.

Chapter in a Page

We approach life either from the head—the rational mind—or from the heart—a place of deep centeredness, where our limbic mind, senses, emotions, instincts, ancestral memories, and intellect come together to guide us. We feel centered within ourselves, content, and clear when we come from our hearts; we do not choose to do it—it is our natural inclination.

Our ego takes over, and we resort to our rational minds, usually in response to fear. The ego controls us through rationale, especially since stress, depression, lack of acknowledgment, insecurity, power struggles, and unfulfilledness are all shades of fear. We aim to ameliorate fear, which leaves us physically and emotionally debilitated. The purpose of the rational mind is to work through what un-centers us and guide us back to the heart.

In our culture we emphasize the rational mind, focusing on freedom of choice and free will. Yet when we come from our heart, there is no choice and no need for free will. The Beauty Way lies before us, our path is given. This does not take away a *right*; it removes a redundancy. Our rational mind fabricates illusory choices. Now we see the simple truth: We must satisfy our needs; there is no choice.

One reason we are emotionally sick is that we have too many choices. Psychological research has shown that having many choices leads to regret, self-blame, a sense of missed opportunity, and unmet expectations. On the other hand, a heart-centered freedom of choice involves conscious steps to foster our maturation and evolve our talents to better care for ourselves and serve our people. Remember, though, the rational mind and the limbic mind are not in competition. Living from the heart means we use our rational mind to serve the limbic mind, not the other way around.

5: We Give Ourselves More Choices Endnotes

1   David Eagleman, *Incognito: The Secret Lives of the Brain* (Vintage, 2012), 8-19.

2   Shirley A. Jones, ed., *Simply Living: The Spirit of the Indigenous People* (New World Library, 1999), 112.

3   Ibid, 150.

4   Randi Gunther, "Too Many Choices," *Psychology Today*, last modified 15 June 2015, accessed 15 October 2020, https://www.psychologytoday.com/blog/rediscovering-love/201506/too-many-choices.

5   Barry Schwartz, "Can There Ever Be Too Many Flowers Blooming?" in *Engaging Art: The Next Great Transformation of America's Cultural Life* (New York: Routledge, 2008), 239-56.

6   Barry Schwartz, *The Paradox of Choice: Why More is Less* (New York: Ecco, 2004), 4.

7   Ibid.

8   Sheena Iyengar and Mark R. Lepper, "When Choice is Demotivating: Can One Desire Too Much of a Good Thing?" *Journal of Personality and Social Psychology* 79, no. 6 (2000): 995.

9   Sheena Iyengar, Gur Huberman and Wei Jiang, "How Much Choice is Too Much? Contributions to 401(k) Retirement Plans," *Pension Design and Structure: New Lessons from Behavioral Finance* (2004): 83-95.

10   "World Happiness Report 2015 Summary," *World Happiness Report*, ed. John Helliwell, Richard Layard, and Jeffrey Sachs, last modified 14 July 2015, accessed October 2020, http://worldhappiness.report/summary/.

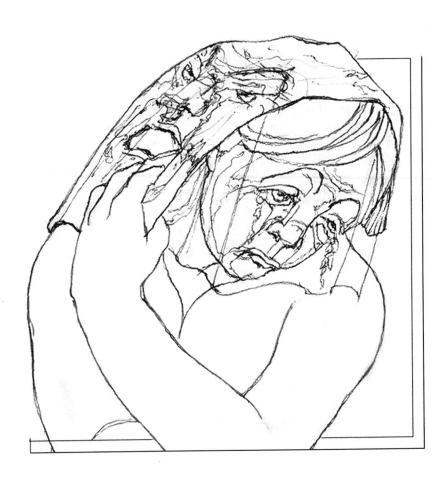

6: We Trust Our Feelings

In *#1*, I mentioned that we can make sense of our two-track mind by framing it in the language of our *thinking self* and our *feeling self*. In this chapter, we look at those selves more closely. We like to think that we are rational beings, guided by intellect. The truth is that we are first emotional beings, then rational ones. We are animals with intellectual capacities.

Our Two Selves

Our feelings alone do not dispense wisdom; it is not the role of feelings to say, "do this," or "don't do that." Feelings tell us what matters to us and what doesn't. Feelings are warning signs of danger or indicators that we are being drawn too close to something and that we risk losing perspective. The rational self is meant to pick up on these signs and guide us back to centeredness by addressing whatever need is represented by these feelings. In this way, the rational mind and the limbic mind work in sync.

We see it daily when feeling follows thought or thought follows feeling. We are thinking *and* feeling, thinking about our feelings and living in the feeling of our thinking—which, you guessed it, can become a bit messy. For many of us, the experience is more entangling than it is poetic. How often have you had trouble thinking clearly when your feelings have gotten in the way? Or had trouble listening to someone else in your emotional state? Or how about the times when you'd like to just be present with a feeling, yet your mental clutter gets in the way?

The first step to disentangling ourselves is to acknowledge that both the feeling self and the thinking self have legitimate voices that can each stand *on their own*. Although the experiences may be somewhat intertwined, we have never gotten very good at giving our feelings rational underpinnings, nor have we been very successful at having our thoughts control our feelings. So we give them equal voice, equal value, and separate attention.

A WORD ABOUT NEEDS

It is best to address a need immediately when it is recognized. All needs are legitimate and require attention; they should not be judged. They are the voice of some aspect of the core self asking the ego self to provide for the wellness of the overall being. When we do not allow ourselves to meet our needs, our ego generates stronger, overpowering feelings to manipulate us and direct our attention to our needs.

We then become needy—an imbalanced state which could lead to imbalanced choices. If neediness becomes chronic, it can result in imbalanced habitual behavior patterns. Then, even though at some point the neediness subsides after the need is met, the habitual behavior persists. Though, more often, the habitual behavior gets in the way of meeting the need in a healthy manner.

We begin by giving voice to the feeling. It is the deeper, more primal impulse that, if we do not express, prevents the full functioning of our intellectual capacities, unbridled from irrational and potentially restrictive feeling. The feeling itself is not inherently irrational, though it becomes irrational when it prevents our rational self from operating fully.

Say I'm angry at my neighbor for driving on my lawn. I could address him first by saying, "I'm really irritated by this tire rut in my front yard, and I want you to know that. At the same time, I don't want it to get in the way of talking with you about the situation. So now that I've expressed my feelings, I'd like to set them aside and check in with you on what actually happened, since I know I don't have the full story."

With virtually all of the patterns and scenarios in this book, both our feeling self and thinking self are involved. If we can separate the two, we see our behavior patterns more clearly—like when expressing emotion alone derails our conflict resolution skills. We can then act more effectively than if we let the two of them talk over each other.

The Myth of Being Primarily Rational

In our culture, we often identify as being either rational or irrational. Our rational mind is the evaluator, of course, so this shows our cultural bias. This is one way that we live from the head instead of the heart. Our mind's view is only a perception. We like to think we are rational creatures, able to clearly view and objectively assess, yet emotions creep into our "rational" evaluations. Consider the following spins we put on things:

1. **Labeling.** You are female, which is why you act that way. I'm lazy, I don't deserve what I'm getting. You're a child, you wouldn't understand.

2. **Distortions.** She's good-looking, she must be an amazing woman. You made a mistake in adding; can't you ever get anything right? He went out and found our lost dog, but it doesn't mean anything coming from a jerk like him.

3. **Shoulda-woulda-couldas.** I should report everything on my taxes. If only she could have tried harder, she'd have made the team. I would have donated something if I had a better paying job.

4. **Taking it personally.** If I didn't have a child, she wouldn't have gotten into that accident. I pay my taxes, and they use it to go bomb women and children to smithereens. If only I were there earlier, I bet I could have prevented that theft.

5. **Inventing facts.** He didn't look at me; he must really think I'm ugly. I never win at raffles, which is why I don't ever buy tickets. I don't have to ask her if she did it; she's just the type of person who steals.

6. **Least common denominator.** No one else is trying very hard, so why should I? Picking up that litter isn't going to do any good; there's so much trash along this road that we'd need a semi-trailer and a crew of twenty people to make any real difference. Sure, I got a raise, but they're probably gonna take it out of my benefits.

7. **Dichotomous perspective.** She's either gonna make a killing or go broke with that new business. If I don't catch something today, I'm never gonna go fishing again. If you're not with me, you're against me.

8. **Defeatism.** I can't even hit the target; I'm never gonna be able to shoot a bow. It was my first time out after my divorce, and I sat alone at a table all night. I might as well get used to it. I couldn't keep a plant alive if I tried.

9. **Feelings create facts.** I feel scared; I'll never be able to ski. I hate Republicans; they must be mean to their kids. You don't like Uncle Jack, and I don't blame you: He thought you were funny looking when you were a baby.

10. **The contamination factor.** That kid's always getting in trouble; I bet the whole family's that way. Ever since you looked at him and smiled, all I can think of is that you're taking every opportunity to get his attention. That meal was terrible; I don't ever want to eat out again.

Many of these emotional spins—and this is only a sampling of them—are posing as rational conclusions. Another way of looking at it is this: There may not always be a rational thought that underpins our feelings, yet there is always a feeling that underpins our supposedly rational thoughts.

Rationality and Feeling

Why have we created a culture that marginalizes feelings? We've gone so far as to call ourselves rational beings, relegating those who would make feeling-based decisions to a weak underclass. It seems as though sharing our feelings has come to mean anything other than actually sharing the feeling. People make careers out of talking, analyzing, singing, and writing about feelings. Why have we become so afraid of raw feeling?

To be fair, we allow women and children their feelings, yet only when relegated to their own worlds. If a woman wants to function in a "man's world," she is told by our culture that she needs to be objective and have full command of her rational capacities, which means setting her feeling self aside. Yet it would be a mistake to even call that *functioning*, as it restricts both men and women from fully experiencing their feelings. It is a world for the purely rational—which none of us are, though we try to live up to the illusion. We convince ourselves or others that what we are doing is based on sound logic. We rewrite emotion in the language of reason, when the two are separate phenomena.

I believe that nearly all the decisions we make are emotionally motivated—and that it would be far healthier for us to admit it and create lives that allow the free and spontaneous expression of feelings rather than having to resort to bar buddies, best friends, and weekly counseling sessions to allow what's going on inside of us to see the light of day. Imagine your whole life being like those precious moments when you feel uninhibited and allow your feelings to freely flow. After all, it is the way of all living things, even us humans—if we could allow ourselves to function as we are designed. Perhaps those blissful moments could become a blissful life.

Words Aren't Feelings

We achieve that bliss when we realize that verbalizing our feelings is not always the answer. Have you ever had an intimate sharing, then had your partner ask, "How did that feel for you?" When you're obviously distraught, do people ask how you're feeling? The rational mind has moved into the territory of feelings—which evolved as a form of nonverbal communication—and reduced them to words. When extremely distraught, we might be given a reprieve, but otherwise, we are expected to come up with words to describe as closely as possible what we feel. Still, it is not the feeling itself.

We are fully capable of communicating and interpreting feelings nonverbally. This ability is innate. Have you ever had to ask a dog to express her feelings? Of course not. Anyone can tell when a dog is angry, happy, anxious, or sad. And we respond accordingly. We don't have to first think about how the dog is feeling. We don't have to consciously listen to the dog's explanation of how she is feeling, and we don't even have to process our observational input. We just know.

Feelings are somatic—they engage the whole body. When we watch the angry dog, we notice her solidly placed feet, tense posture, stiffened tail, and raised hackles. Then we notice her face, with head down, ears laid back, and lips curled. We listen to the low rumble rising from her throat. Every fiber of that dog's being speaks *anger*.

Now imagine going up to her and asking, "How are you feeling?" Wouldn't that be silly? Maybe even provocative? Even if she could answer verbally, would words equally capture what she was telling you somatically? The same is true with us humans. We are animals just as much as dogs are, and we can express and read each other's feelings in the same way.

When we express our feelings verbally, we disconnect from our feeling core, which is our limbic process (also known as the *mammalian mind*). Its operating system uses the language common to all life, which is nonverbal. As soon as we start talking, we engage the rational mind, which knows nothing about feelings, so it stumbles around to find words to express them. It's like lifting a fish out of the water and asking her to describe how she was swimming rather than just leaving her be and watching her do it.

Here's what we can do the next time someone asks us to express our feelings:

1. Don't go to your head.
2. Become your inner dog.
3. Don't fight it—allow yourself to fully embody what you are feeling.
4. Let it course through your veins and shape your body.
5. Let it paint your face and taint your voice.
6. Now you are expressing your feelings!

How Emotions Hook Us

Emotions evolved to impassion the moment. They last only ninety seconds or so,[1] then they dissipate. When they endure, they transform into a *mood* rather than a discrete emotional experience.[2, 3] If I'm startled by a strange noise, a wave of fear and a rush of adrenaline instantly have me at the peak of my strength and awareness. However, if the fear were to persist beyond the event, my adrenaline level would stay elevated and I'd remain on edge—a debilitating state of being.

Think of a feeling as a cloud rolling over the sun. Clouds come in all shapes and sizes: Some are wispy and some are dense, some are dark and some are light. Yet they all drift by, and the sun again shines.

Unless the ego hooks them. When our ego isn't content with a feeling just coming and going, he drops a hook down from the rational mind and attempts to snag the feeling. If he is successful, he hoists the feeling up from the heart into our frontal lobes and starts processing it. Once we hook a feeling, it becomes an attachment. The rational mind can keep processing the "feeling" for a long time. Have you ever felt jealous or resentful, and you just couldn't get it off of your mind? The reason is it was literally *in your mind*. That passing cloud expanded and became an overcast sky.

Why does the ego do this? The main reason is fear. Whenever we are threatened in any way, the ego takes charge. This fear-driven ego trusts nobody, not even his bosom brother, the limbic process, which is the cradle of our feelings. He has to be in control—it's his job to protect us. This is why he hijacks feelings and commandeers the rational mind to process and express them. The end result is verbal (and often assertive) expression.

Usually we end up feeling worse than before, as we did not experience the full-body release that comes from expressing a feeling somatically. We feel incomplete and unfulfilled, so the ego again steps in, and he attempts to rescue us by giving us more of the same. We ask, "How are you feeling?" more often, and we make more of an effort to verbally, rather than organically and somatically, express our feelings to others.

Often it becomes a patterned behavior, and we begin experiencing chronic stress since we are never left feeling fulfilled. Some of us sink into periodic depression. Others look for emotional release in other ways: through medication, psychotherapy, emotionally stimulating experiences, and sometimes abusive practices—all the result of losing touch with the animal we are. Pure, somatically expressed feelings do not—and cannot—lie. An angry dog is an angry dog. Period.

Focusing Too Much on Feeling

When we know the reason for emotions and how they work, we no longer have to be victimized by the underlying beliefs and patterns that trigger our emotional responses or moods. To focus wholly on the emotion in an effort to get out from under a debilitating emotional state can only result in a temporary fix. As much as the ego's hooks lead us to become fixated on a feeling, the real issue is the conviction or behavior that keeps inviting the feeling back. Emotional healing, then, rests on changing my belief system and adopting new relationship patterns.

With overpowering feelings such as anger and jealousy, the standard healing approach is to focus on the feeling itself rather than its cause. Therapists teach a few anger management techniques, then send the client back out in the world to cope. I'm not implying that there's anything inherently wrong with this approach, as I see the clear and immediate benefit in giving someone with a broken leg a crutch.

Yet, why the broken leg in the first place? With the crutch, did we just enable the person to go out and break the other leg, or maybe break the same leg twice? After a while, they might get used to walking with crutches; they may even forget what it's like to walk without them.

For those of us who are dwelling in woundedness rather than healing, the core emotions we have in play are fear and longing. Just like our thinking and feeling selves, they turn out to be strange bedfellows, as fear keeps us from satisfying our longing. We experience longing due to unmet needs, which keeps us fearful of never having those needs met. The ego then steps in to protect us from being hurt, with the resulting boundaries, defensiveness, and dysfunctional behavioral patterns—what I call our nobility—making it all the less likely that we are able to satisfy our longings.

Nobility is a splendid performance: It is living a life that is, in many ways, removed from life as it actually is. It is the monarch, sitting coddled in the castle since it is his *divine right* as king. It is us, acting out of alignment with our hearts and telling ourselves it is *for our own good*. Unmasking our nobility would be an exercise in stark honesty—a courageous look behind the self-protective wall we have built. Perhaps the first step would be to admit that the wall exists, as it appears to me that most of us function under the illusion that our wall is our authentic personality.

The Illusion of Objectivity

Rather than there being an objective reality, we create reality through a subjective, feeling-tempered lens. Take the case of Genghis Khan, who created the world's most extensive empire in only twenty-five years—more than the Romans could accomplish in hundreds. Our "objective" assessment of Genghis's accomplishments typically paints him as a ruthless conqueror. However, there is an inside story few know: He rid his domain of the feudal system and aristocratic privilege, he abolished torture, and he granted religious freedom. Cultural exchange, trade, and the arts blossomed like never before. In these respects, he far outshone his Asian and European counterparts. As for the ruthless Khan himself, I have yet to talk with a person who knows that he was a loving husband, married to a Christian, and had many Christians, Daoists, Buddhists, and Muslims in his court.[4]

We all have our beliefs and blind spots that keep us from seeing what is right in front of us, even though we are looking. This is the premise of optical illusions: We are convinced we're seeing one thing, until we realize we're actually seeing something else. We have blind spots since we each have only one subjective perspective. Once we recognize this, it becomes impossible to say *always* or *never* again. There are no more answers, only questions that beget questions that beget questions.

Yet our broader culture and our personal nobility prefer certainty—and an acculturated value of ours, objectivity, helps preserve certainty. Like nobility, it requires us to ignore our own Truth for the sake of a supposedly grander, better, truer reality. Unfortunately, objectivity, as we understand it, only gets us further from our healing.

Our culture tells us we can see the world either through impartial observations and clear, objective thinking—or through subjective viewpoints, clouded thoughts, and biases. We treat objective as good and subjective as, well, perhaps not *bad*, but certainly not good. We treat objective as revelatory and subjective as grounds for dismissal—many of us complain about biased news reporting, prejudiced judiciaries, and people with slanted points of view.

Our opinions are based on the belief that there is such a thing as objectivity. We tend to consider the thoughts and beliefs that we agree with to be objective and anything else to be biased and emotionally based. We hold each other up to the litmus test of objectivity, when we are not capable of it ourselves.

After all, how can there be any objectivity when all that we perceive and express has to pass through our personal filter? There can, then, be no objective truth, no clear thinking, no unbiased actions. The mere fact that I would label something objective implies that it has passed through my filter and been given my judgment—its objectivity has become my, or my community's, subjective interpretation.

In all of its guises—impartiality, nondiscrimination, unbiased, etc.—objectivity is created by agreement. If you and I agree on a moral code, we can be part of a "fair and impartial" jury. If you and I agree to a mathematical approach to the universe, we can begin "objectively" observing and recording data. If we can agree on what constitutes life, we can make objective assessments on everything from abortion to what we eat.

What that leaves us with is a socially accepted objectivity. It calls itself *objectivity*, when it is simply whatever has been deemed socially acceptable. So often, I see cries for objectivity as no more than thinly veiled coercion to conform to some status quo. As soon as we attach words to something, we have lost the opportunity to be objective. Whether we choose to describe someone as rich or poor, or by ethnicity, or religion, is a reflection of what we value. Whether or not we even choose to address a particular topic is a clear statement of what we value. I contend that every thought, feeling, word, and action is laden with personal prejudice.

Objectivity and Feelings

Inspired by the illusion of objectivity versus subjectivity, we have created for ourselves a dichotomous world—things are either black and white, right or wrong, hurtful or helpful. We are either at work or on vacation, we are either vegetarians or meat-eaters, we are either telling the truth or lying. Life is reduced to a simple matter of choice: All we need to do is slip everything—including our self—into its proper category, and we have done our job.

When it comes to communication, it is commonly perceived that the sharing of feelings is subjective, and observations and rational conclusions are objective. People striving to make their communication more conscious and less likely to trigger the listener work to separate their feelings from their truth, or their observations from their judgments, the premise being that the objective is more conducive to clear communication than the subjective. "Is that an observation or a judgment?" someone might ask. Or, "can you separate your truth from your feeling?"

Yet it is not possible for us to speak or listen, to see or hear, to feel or think objectively. We cannot merely observe. Any personal input or output, no matter in what guise, is subjective. It all goes through my filters, which are by nature limiting and/or expanding, magnifying, coloring, distorting, prioritizing, and so on, *ad infinitum*.

To claim objectivity in my emotional expression would be a denial of the self—even a denial that the self exists. There are no objective observations, assessments, or data. There are no objective facts, truths, or judgments. Every thought and feeling I have, every desire and impulse, is biased. It is biased in that it is my own—which is the only thing it should be.

The illusions of nobility and objectivity are of the mind. The path of the Beauty Way is of the heart. In words attributed to the Buddha (in the sixth century BCE): "The world and all that is in it is a construct of my mind. What I am is created by my thoughts. The life I lead is scripted by my thoughts. When I speak or act from my mind, turmoil follows in the same way the cart wheel follows the foot of the ox. When I speak or act from my heart, serenity follows as unfailingly as my faithful shadow."[5]

Objectivity and Truth

So what about truth? I believe it still exists; however, only on a personal level. Each of us has our own truth, which is necessarily subjective and applies only to us and only to the moment at hand (for more on this topic, see my book *Truthspeaking: Ancestral Ways to Hear and Speak the Voice of the Heart*). Details and arguments cannot support our truth, as they have no relationship to it. The moment's truth is found in the voice of our heart.

It is only when we worship objectivity that we begin to think that truth is a zero-sum game: that if my truth is different from yours, then one of us is living in untruth. When we acknowledge that life is subjective, we recognize there can be many truths and that this plurality makes our lives richer.

If we are sincere about wanting to live in honor and respect, we must do more than pay lip service to another's truth—we must make space for it to coexist with ours. It takes humility, which comes from admitting that our truth is biased and limited. It also takes courage and self-awareness to say that I am looking for a truth that is true to me—*that* perspective is truly countercultural, and it is what brings us closer to living in alignment with our core self.

Embracing the subjectivity of life gives us permission to hold our personal truth and our core self up to the light. Rather than hiding behind some lofty-sounding phantom ideal, let us speak our hearts with each other. And let us listen. The imperative to agree or disagree fades away. Instead of one truth, one assessment of reality, there are as many as there are people to express them. Instead of conforming to some commonly held ideal or belief, we listen to our dreams and the guiding voices that speak directly to each of us.

Chapter in a Page

We like to identify as rational beings, guided by intellect. The truth is we are first emotional beings, with intellectual capacities in a supportive role. Our emotions signify our core needs, and the rational self guides us back to centeredness by addressing those needs; the rational mind and the limbic mind work in sync. Our thinking and feeling selves often get entangled, so we must give them equal voice and separate attention.

First, express the feeling. It is the more primal impulse that, when ignored, inhibits our intellectual capacities. A feeling is not inherently irrational; it becomes that way when it stymies our rational self. Challenge the bias against fully expressing raw feelings. Prolonged, chronic, and unaddressed emotions are debilitating, usually due to underlying beliefs or patterned behaviors that keep triggering the same emotional response.

The myth of our essential rationality has a sister myth: objectivity. Our culture emphasizes impartial observations and clear, objective thinking—and derides subjective viewpoints and biases. Yet how can objectivity exist when all we perceive and express has to pass through our personal filter? We wrongly call personal assessments subjective and observations objective. In fact, every thought and feeling I have is biased, as I cannot experience them without my subjective self. Furthermore, to claim objectivity in my emotional expression would be a denial of the self. What passes for objectivity, then, is whatever is deemed socially acceptable.

Embracing the subjectivity of life reveals our personal truth and our core self. Rather than hiding behind some phantom ideal, let us speak our hearts. And let us listen. The imperative to agree or disagree fades away. Instead of one truth, one assessment of reality, there are as many as there are people to express them. Instead of conforming to some commonly held ideals or beliefs, we listen to our dreams and the guiding voices that speak directly to each of us.

6: We Trust Our Feelings Endnotes

1   Jill Bolte Taylor, *My Stroke of Insight* (Penguin Books, 2009), 146.

2   Klaus Scherer and Paul Ekman, *Approaches to Emotion* (Hillsdale, NJ: L. Erlbaum Associates, 1984), 333.

3   Paul Ekman and Richard J. Davidson, *The Nature of Emotion: Fundamental Questions* (New York: Oxford UP, 1994), 51

4   Jack Weatherford, *Genghis Khan and the Making of the Modern World* (Three Rivers Press, 2004), 58.

5   Rendered in contemporary vernacular by the author from the following texts:
    Thomas Byrom, *Dhammapada: The Sayings of the Buddha* (Shambala, 1993).
    John Ross Carter, *The Dhammapada: The Sayings of the Buddha* (Oxford, 2000).
    Thomas Cleary, *Dhammapada: The Sayings of Buddha* (Bantam Books, 1995).
    Thich Nhat Hanh, *The Dhammapada* (Parallax Press, 2005).
    Harischandra Kaviratna, *Dhammapada: Wisdom of the Buddha* (Oxford, 1980).
    Juan Mascar, *The Dhammapada* (Penguin, 1973).
    Max Müller, *The Dhammapada* (Oxford: Clarendon Press, 1881).
    Glen Wallis, *The Dhammapada: Verses on the Way* (Modern Library, 2004).

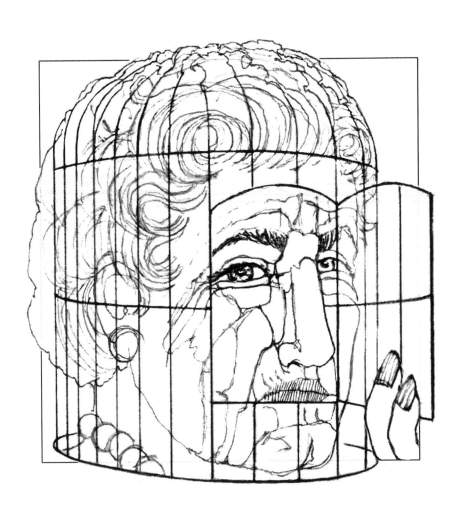

7: We Let Fear Control Us

Once more you stand at the edge of the familiar pond in the woods, the same pond where you contemplated the meaning of boundaries. Its surface is now speckled here and there with drops of rain. The branches of an old Cedar provide a dry spot to stand absorbed in thought as the words of an Elder ripple through your mind: "How can I overcome fear?" you had asked; and the Elder replied, "By being like a raindrop that falls from the sky, unshackled and untroubled by where it should fall."

You draw a sense of inspiration from standing in the memory of those words and the animated pitter-patter around you. The tickle of mosquito bites eventually brings you back to the moment. The rain has stopped; the amber light of the setting sun glows on the pond's surface.

Leaving behind the shelter of the Cedar, you begin to retrace your path through the woods in the night. You remind yourself that it is not the dark you are afraid of—it is the unknown that may be in it. The snapping of twigs not far ahead disrupts this meditation. You look off to the side and discern a Bear ambling in your direction. The thought of death by mauling immediately consumes your conscious mind.

For a split second, though, you wonder, "How accurate is that? Do I see a Death-by-Mauling, or do I see a Bear? If I remain centered and come from my Heart-of-Hearts, I see only a Bear." You remember the raindrops and step back from your rational mind and allow yourself to be guided by your limbic mind, which has been around Bears much longer. Instead of reacting, you are *as a question,* and you observe: Is she with cubs? Has she seen me? Are our paths going to cross? Might she just pass through without ever noticing me? And if so, does it matter?

You are still afraid, yet you are no longer consumed by fear, and it is this distinction that makes all the difference. You find yourself able to see Bear first as a sister and fellow woodswalker rather than as a threat. You remain on alert—even as her presence no longer victimizes you. She passes on her way, and so do you, though instead of moving in fear, you move with an evolved awareness and even a sense of empathy for Bear.

The Vital Difference between Fear and Being Afraid

When we think of fear, what comes to mind? For most people I talk with, it is fear of a person, event, or thing, such as a rapist, an out-of-control car, a terrible storm, or a wild animal. In other words, when we are asked about fear, we tend to respond by speaking about fear *of* something—which is a projection of our fear rather than the fear itself.

Those projections dwell in the rational mind, and they are used by the ego to throw up quick boundaries in an effort to protect us. When I stumble across a Bear in the woods and think *death by mauling,* it's not my ego maliciously antagonizing me—it's my ego conjuring an image in my mind in order to elicit a quick response that aids my survival. Beneath this projection—or any projection of our fear—is the real feeling: that of *being afraid.*

This feeling dwells in the limbic mind, along with our other core feelings of longing, sadness, and joy. Since the limbic mind is the seat of our core feelings, it is also where we receive the wisdom to address them. The limbic mind holds deep, ancestral memories that guide our intuitive and instinctive behaviors. It is the seat of nonverbal communication and the place of deep knowing that transcends whatever is going on in our ego-based surface reality. It is the seat of honor and respect, of Circle Consciousness and empathy. Responding to fear from the limbic mind means we experience being afraid without being consumed by it, in a way that brings us into relationship with our surroundings.

CIRCLE CONSCIOUSNESS

When we live as one voice with those of our clan, then we are living with Circle Consciousness. *One voice* does not mean a homogenous voice—it is an integrative one that we arrive at by speaking and listening from the heart, by listening to the voices of everyone and taking them all to heart. When I act from Circle Consciousness, I no longer see myself as an isolated individual; instead, I recognize my place alongside all my Relations.

In the example of the Bear, the ego tells us *death by mauling*, and we can either listen to this message or react to it. When we listen to the ego, we can extract the truth of the moment—you may be in danger, and you need to be prepared to act to save your life—and consult our limbic mind accordingly. If we react instead, then we respond from a place of preconceived notions, prejudices, and projections: We scream, we run away, or we shoot the Bear. Reacting to the ego means I would only be reinforcing my stereotype, and I would have learned nothing about this particular Bear or Bears in general. I might even lose my life. Either way, I would have missed the opportunity to evolve my awareness and relationship skills.

Knowing Our Fear

Whether you call it *fear* or *being afraid*, it has nothing to do with any particular person, event, or thing. It is simply a lack of knowing. It is only the rational mind that distinguishes one fear from another. So, the solution is in the definition: We get over our fear by coming to know it. The critical point to remember is that "it" is not *what* we fear, that is only a projection; we must understand fear itself.

What follows is the five-step approach I use. It goes by the acronym AAPRR.

Step 1: Attune. I acknowledge and recognize my fear by introducing myself to it, and it to me, just as though I were meeting a new person.

Step 2: Assess. Is this a familiar fear or a new one? What degree of fear am I experiencing? Are other people affected?

Step 3: Perspective. What do I gain or lose by working with this fear? What have I gained or lost in the past by not working with it?

Step 4: Respond. The most effective way is to embrace it. If the fear is too big and bad to embrace alone, reach out for help and support.

Step 5: Release. The bitter edge of fear usually dissipates with Step 4. Now I can release myself from it by fully digesting it, and in doing so, it transforms from my nemesis into my guide.

Now, rather than being victimized by my fear, I'm on the same wavelength with it. Instead of it staring me in the face, we're looking out from the same vantage point and working together.

FINDING WHAT WORKS FOR YOU

There are many, many fear-management techniques other than AAPRR, which range from cognitive therapy to direct emotional release. So whether it's working with a counselor, talking with a friend, punching a pillow, or digging a hole and screaming into it, the important thing is to find something that works for you. Most techniques take you up to Step 3. From there, you can move to Steps 4 and 5 above to complete the process.

Fear and Projections of Fear

Once there was a Seeker and an Elder who were traveling together. While passing through a village, they came upon a building with the front door left open invitingly. The young woman walked in, and in no more than the time it took her to turn around, she came flying back out to the street.

"There was a group of women in the building," she stammered, "and right away they turned angry and fearful looking! This town must be filled with hateful people."

"Come with me back into the building," the Elder replied, "and show me what you saw. You need not fear, for I will enter first."

There, where each of the wrathful women had been standing, the Seeker now saw a kindly person wearing a gentle smile and holding out a hand in greeting. Bewildered, the Seeker followed the Elder back onto the street.

"I do not understand," muttered the Seeker. "A minute ago I wanted to leave this town as fast as my feet would carry me, and now I feel welcomed and would like to stay for a while."

"What we give, we receive back one hundredfold," the Elder stated. "This is a mirror shop, and the only thing the shopkeeper has to sell is his customer's reflection."

You may have heard the saying, *there is nothing to fear but fear itself.* It refers to the projections of our fear that feed our imagination and haunt our memories. As we saw with the case of the Bear, the fearful projections are meant to throw up a boundary to protect us—yet often they overwhelm us before we get a chance to put up that boundary.

As happened with the Seeker, we begin to lose perspective. The projections of our fear make us reactive, muffle our Truth, sabotage relationships, and leave us constantly on alert. They blind and cripple us—which leaves us incapable of being fully present and engaging in relationship.

It is the projections of our fear that victimize us, not the fear itself. Fear is generic. No matter what triggers it and no matter how we might react to it, it is all based on the same fear. Think of fear as a crossroads with vehicles—the triggering events—entering from several different directions. The vehicles leaving this crossroads in many directions represent our various reactions to fear. The roads themselves are our patterns—they are what cause the initial event to trigger fear in us, then what causes our fear to trigger a specific reaction.

The cars and the roads are each part of the experience of the crossroads, yet they are not the crossroads itself. The same is true of fear: The triggering events, reactions, and behavioral patterns related to fear are part of how we experience it, although they are not the emotion itself.

Fear is vital to living in Balance. When we mix up fear with projections of fear, it's easy to then look at the list of our core emotions—fear, longing, sadness, and joy—and say, "I don't care at all for the first three, but I sure like experiencing joy." The truth is, we need all four of them for our well-being. Without longing, we would have no motivation, and without sadness, there would be no introspection. Without fear to guide us, it is doubtful we would be able to survive for long.

Many of us think that we can retreat to a safe place to protect ourselves from fear. However, that is an illusion, as in effect what we have done is imprison ourselves in fear. It's the same as thinking we protect ourselves from drowning by ignoring the fact that our boat is slowly filling with water. Pretending that the fear or its trigger isn't happening does not make them disappear.

Fear is part of our core nature: Where we go, it goes. Only by embracing our fear do we live in Balance with fear as our guide, not our master. When we acknowledge that the boat is sinking and we are afraid, we can then act in a way that promotes our survival. It is our fear that guides us to put on our life vest, attempt to plug the leak in the hull, and radio to shore for help.

Fear and Healing

The standard healing approach in our culture is to work on our fear as though it were something that doesn't belong, something that is wrong with us. This approach leads us to fight our core selves. If I were to embrace my fears, experience them viscerally, and know them intimately, then I could see through the images I have created around them, right into what they really are: a natural response from my limbic mind meant to kick-start my survival instinct.

Fear can be healthy: You don't have to slide into victimization mode in order to survive. Contrary to what our culture tells us, we can listen to fear and get the message in an empowered way.

Many healing approaches to fear-based victimization focus on the triggering event or on the reaction that the event triggers. To return to the crossroads example, they respond to an influx of traffic jams, fender-benders, and collisions by looking at the cars; they forget to question whether the roads are uneven, full of potholes, or lack signage. The cars are only as good as the roads they're driven on. There are always triggering events; what leads us to fear, and then to reactive behaviors, are the patterns we have established by trying in vain to cope with situations beyond our ability.

Here are five steps to manage fear:

1. **Recognize** that *fear* is the core emotion. Anger, aggressiveness, and submission are no more than shades of fear.

2. **Realize** that these secondary reactions to fear are not natural responses; they are the result of unhealthy patterns we have developed to cope with fear.

3. **Focus** on establishing healthy new patterns based on self-awareness and *Truthspeaking* (the old patterns naturally fall by the wayside and dissipate for lack of attention).

4. **Embrace** fear as an ally. It is our warning light that we have inadequately dealt with a triggering event and we are now in danger of succumbing to our reactive pattern.

5. **Acknowledge** that fear is no more than a lack of knowing. This is our springboard to coming to know ourselves so that we can develop a healthy pattern of being with our differences.

We revert to patterned behaviors when we are not living in the now. Our patterned behaviors are us reliving memories. And those behaviors started between the ages of zero and three. When we're triggered, our mind reaches back, back, back to find a behavioral pattern that's going to meet the trigger in a way that promotes our survival. That goes way back into our reptilian brain—the limbic mind—that sits right at the top of our spinal column. That's where all our memories are stored from ages zero to three.

At that age, we responded to fear only from the limbic mind, so it's not our rational process at all. The rational mind comes next, though, when the reptilian brain throws the behavioral pattern into our frontal lobes, into our rational brain, to design a blueprint for action.

With the limbic and rational minds in sync, now we can embrace our fear and do something about it instead of being a slave to it. If we were reptiles, operating without a neocortex, we wouldn't have any semblance of choice. Referring back to #5, when it comes to fear, the only real *choice* we have is the one that best meets our needs: embracing the fear and letting it guide us.

When we do that, we are acting from the Heart-of-Hearts and asking: What do I know? What or who can help me? Can I listen to my intuition here? Maybe I have some Elders I can consult. What are my feelings telling me? That's what I mean by embracing your fear. It means living in the present, fully conscious and aware. Perhaps most importantly for those of us who have had a poor relationship with fear, when we embrace it, we allow our rational mind to focus on addressing it instead of creating projections.

WOUNDEDNESS AND CORE EMOTIONS

We who struggle with self-identity are driven predominately by two of the core emotions: fear and longing. They work in collusion to keep us crippled—fear keeps us from satisfying our longing, and the inability to satisfy our longing keeps us in fear of being authentic in our relationships. Whether it's codependency, victimization-enabling, or control issues, all are responses to fear. The core fear is fear of abandonment.

Staying Present When Fear Takes Over

Fear typically takes one of three forms, based on our fight-flight-freeze mechanism:

- **Fighting** can take the form of arguing, getting defensive, criticizing, and creating alliances.
- **Fleeing** usually amounts to diversionary behaviors, turning to drugs, alcohol, or fantasies, or literally fleeing.
- **Freezing** most often takes the form of shutting down.

Whichever option we resort to, the bottom line is that we are reacting and are no longer present in the moment. In our cultural narrative about fear, we often overlook this point, even though it is an important aspect of how we respond to fear.

If possible, stay present with fear. When we start resorting to any of the three options listed, we begin to develop a patterned behavioral response, which becomes our fallback reaction to fear. We develop neural channels in our brain that automatically have us arguing, fleeing, or shutting down when we are confronted with fear. It's as predictable as flicking on a switch, which makes us act more like robots than conscious, engaged beings. Ultimately, there is no better pattern to have with fear than to be present in it.

Below I have provided several ways to stay present during stressful situations. Each is a biofeedback technique that is easy to execute in the moment. *Biofeedback* refers to any method of gaining some measure of voluntary control over a biological function. In this case, we are stimulating specific parts of the body to exert control over our fear. All we have to do is practice these techniques so that we can put our trust in them and have them at our disposal when needed.

The techniques below work since they bring sensation and blood flow back to the extremities, including the head and brain. When our fight-flight-freeze mechanism is triggered, we go into survival mode, which means that we lose touch with our extremities—brain included—while we focus on protecting our torso. The following methods draw conscious energy back to our extremities, which reactivates them and enables us to return to a state of full-being consciousness.

Return-to-Consciousness Techniques

- **Hand Heat.** Imagine you are on a beach and digging your hands into the hot sand, or that you are washing your hands in hot water. Feel the sensation of the heat, and notice your hands warming.

- **Thumb Pinch.** Squeeze the soft tissue between your thumb and forefinger until you feel mild pain. Hold until you notice yourself again becoming conscious of your extremities.

- **Toe Crunch.** Curl your toes tight to the count of ten, release, then repeat. You can achieve the same by tightening your calf or thigh muscles.

- **Pulse Connect.** At your wrist, elbow, neck, temple, or groin, feel your pulse. Monitor it until you are reconnected with your total being.

- **Aroma Jolt.** Inhale a stimulating essence, such as peppermint, tea tree, or eucalyptus essential oil. Put a drop on your wrist, a piece of cloth, or your upper lip.

Suicide: The Extreme of Chronic Fear

When the fear state becomes chronic, it typically manifests passively as depression and actively through self-destructive tendencies. In the extreme, either manifestation can result in people becoming actively suicidal (which means not just discussing or reflecting on it but engaging in the process). If you ever find yourself or someone else in such a state, seek professional help immediately. *Do not trust in your ability to handle the situation*, as the mind of a suicidal person usually functions counterintuitively.

WARNING!

Many people commit suicide when you least expect it. A wave of peace comes over them, which causes you to relax and think the crisis is over. However, the state of calm results from the victim coming to clarity that suicide is the route to take. Do two things: Stay with the person—do not leave him/her alone for one second—and get professional help at once.

When it is not possible to get immediate help, here are your two best options:

1. **Cool the brain.** When people are actively suicidal, it's beyond the time for problem-solving. You need to get them into survival mode, which means getting them out of their heads and into their core bodies. This is best accomplished by doing the *reverse* of the biofeedback techniques we just covered. You want to activate the fight-flight-freeze mechanism, which is all about survival. Do it quickly and effectively by placing something cold, such as an ice pack, on the forehead. Use whatever is immediately at hand, as time is of the essence and you need to stay with the person. I once used snow when I tracked down a suicide case. The way cooling down works is that rational processing slows, and the limbic process—which is survival-oriented—takes over. The extremities follow suit by sending their energy to the torso to support its survival.

2. **Lie.** There is a saying amongst mental health crisis workers that *all is fair in love, war, and suicide prevention.* Scruples mean nothing to a dead person, so if a lie can save a life, many crisis workers decide to fabricate or deceive. I heard one person put it this way: "I'll tell them anything—and I mean anything—they want to hear. If someone is ready to jump and says she needs to talk to Brad Pitt, I tell her that I got ahold of him and he's on hold, and all she needs to do is come down and get the phone."

Chapter in a Page

Most people think of fear as tied to a person, event, or thing, although only the rational mind distinguishes one fear from another. When we speak about fear *of* something, it is a projection of our fear rather than the emotion itself.

Fear, or *being afraid*, is simply a lack of knowing. This means we move through it by understanding it. We then experience being afraid without being consumed by its projections, which brings us into better relationship with our surroundings.

The projections of fear, not the feeling, victimize us. Those projections dwell in the rational mind, and the ego uses them to throw up quick boundaries to protect us. Too often the projections overwhelm us before we can respond to them.

Fear is a core emotion—along with longing, sadness, and joy—vital to living in Balance. We need all four for our well-being. Without longing, we lack motivation; without sadness, there's no introspection. Without fear to guide us, we probably wouldn't survive for long.

Our culture approaches fear as though it were something wrong with us. This leads us to fight our core selves. Instead we must acknowledge our fear, embrace it, and learn from it by remaining present and not blindly reacting to it.

When we resort to the fight-flight-freeze mechanism to deal with fear, we begin to develop a patterned behavior. Our hardwired neural channels automatically have us arguing, fleeing, or shutting down. It's like flicking on a switch, making us more like robots than conscious, engaged beings. Ultimately, the best pattern to have with fear is to be present in it.

When fear becomes chronic, it typically manifests passively as depression and actively through self-destructive tendencies. In the extreme, either manifestation can result in people becoming actively suicidal. If ever you find yourself or someone else in such a state, seek professional help immediately.

8: We Believe in Mental Illness

The next three chapters ask you to take a hard look at specific beliefs that underpin how our culture views and handles woundedness. First, I'd like to revisit what this book is and what it is not. This book is not a New Age gospel. It is not a charlatan's cure. It is not my perch to sing from, and it is not a product: It is a perspective. What you are getting here is the essence of what I have learned from a lifetime with traditional healers, contemporary therapists, and the animals I have lived with. This book is an attempt to pass along their wisdom so that you may approach life from a place of healing, not woundedness.

In order to do that, we must be willing to rethink our culture's most sacred concepts. For many of us in the Western world, this kind of self-reflection can seem blasphemous—and it is. It is vital for our healing to *be as a question* in the most fundamental way: by calling *into question* what we have received as objective truth. As we saw in #6, objectivity itself, one of the hallmarks of Western culture, is less sound than we've been led to believe.

Calling into question cultural beliefs doesn't mean we open Pandora's box. The box is already open. Questioning our cultural precepts brings us closer to resolving our woundedness, to containing the chaos. As Jiddu Krishnamurti said, "It is no measure of health to be well adjusted to a profoundly sick society."[1] By conforming to contemporary beliefs about woundedness, we keep ourselves sick.

The premise I function from is that we humans are nature, and if we are going to return to Balance with ourselves and our world, we have to do it nature's way—which is not necessarily the way espoused by Western culture. All that I present in this book has been run countless times through two filters: the people I work with and nature. If something passes through one and not the other, I do not consider it to be compatible with our intrinsic makeup.

One premise of this book is that we take an active role in maintaining our wellness by addressing the sometimes-subconscious assumption that we don't already possess what it takes to lead vibrant, healthy lives. Perhaps the most important place that we enact this assumption is in our very concept of *mental illness*. We don't bat an eyelash at the term these days. In this chapter, we discuss how belief in this concept leads us to see ourselves as mentally ill, which keeps us sick and dependent.

The Myth of Mental Illness

Mental illness is distinct from a physical injury to the brain, an anatomical abnormality of the brain, and the deterioration of the brain due to a pathogen. Mental illness brings us into the realm of the less tangible *mind* and *self,* not simply the physical organ of the brain or the body. As psychologist Thomas Szasz describes it, we have taken the problems of living and turned them into the specter of an "illness"—in other words, we treat people's eccentricities, and even their core emotions, as illnesses and try to make them go away.[2]

When we speak of the *myth of mental illness,* that does not mean we are overlooking or ignoring a person's behavior, reactions, or personality. It means that we deconstruct the way that these things have become labeled signs of *illness* and *disease.* Moving beyond the myth involves moving beyond the ways we judge what or who is different as bad, inferior, or sick.

The concept of mental illness is a social phenomenon that is anchored to our belief in objectivity. It entails the labeling of a person's subjective experience of self and world as *delusional* or symptomatic of a *disorder*—as something that contradicts the "objective" truth of the way things are.

Consider: A woman enters a clinic and states that she is a Bear and is seeking refuge from a man hunting her in the woods; her diagnosis as delusional is based on an "objective" social judgment that she is neither a Bear nor being hunted in the woods. What is important is not what the patient perceives; it is the *method* by which she is diagnosed with an "illness."

Szasz notes that we make evaluations about a person's physical health based on the functioning of their organs, yet the question of what makes a person's *mind* "functioning" or "ill" is less clear.[3] In response, our culture has crafted legal and social definitions of what constitutes an ill mind. Notably, even though some of these definitions have been deleted and criticized as biased (as in the case of women's hysteria or homosexuality in the twentieth century), the diagnostic method is still regarded as "objective."[4, 5, 6, 7] We ask people with subjective lives and perspectives to objectively evaluate others using "objective" definitions made by subjective people.

The concept of mental illness is built on subjective perspective—yet this is precisely the thing that is dismissed in matters of mental illness, since only one kind of subjectivity matters here: that of the observer. A person who is *unhealthy*, who has a bodily organ that is injured or does not function, may still self-describe as being "well"—and that perspective is socially acceptable. However, in the case of a person who is *mentally ill* and self-describes as "well," the self-description is taken as an indication that the person is *not* well. When a person's subjective perspective conflicts with the majority, it is described as wrong to a pathological degree. We discuss a case study of this effect in the coming pages.

The Role of the Ego

In order to fully understand the rise of the concept of mental illness in our culture, we need to understand the way that the ego and the dichotomous mind have shaped the way we perceive ourselves and the world around us.

The ego and the dichotomous mind draw lines of separation. The first is between self and others—the creation of an *I* and a *you*. Once that first line is drawn between self and others, two things happen. First, more lines appear—life and death, justice and injustice, sickness and wellness, and so on. Second, once the illusion of self is created, it naturally follows that the ego creates a myth that something is not just different, there's also something wrong with the self in relation to others. When I see my suffering as strictly mine, then notice that another does not appear to be suffering, I conclude that wellness lies beyond me; so in accordance with the dichotomy, I must be sick.

Every line drawn by the ego has a shared narrative: It is defined between two points, a beginning and an end, balancing delicately on a midpoint. In one case, life is the start, death is the end, and you stand either on the side of life or death. Since the ego is enveloped in the dichotomous mind, it is constantly comparing and evaluating, as it needs to know whether things fall on one side of the line or the other. Something is always right, and something is always wrong—if it is *right*, it cannot be wrong, and if it is *wrong*, it cannot be right.

We transpose this formula onto our lived realities. We see the experience of an illness, like the flu, and the process of healing as having a start and an end. There is also a *correct* direction to the narrative: We start sick, and we end healed. We also see the sickness itself and the state of being sick as positioned on the *wrong* side of the line.

In the same way, we view the internal mental imbalances we were given to walk with as a sickness, with a distinct time of origin and—hopefully—a distinct time when it ceases. We are typically not grateful for our imbalances; we do not see the blessings that we would receive from working with them. Due to the dichotomous mind, when we are told the imbalance is a sickness, we are also implicitly told that it cannot be a sign of wellness. So rather than working to receive those blessings, we work for the day when we become free of imbalances—when we cross over to the right side of the line. For this reason, we go through life under the illusion that we are sick, and we never get well.

Misdiagnoses and Inventions

The problem with this narrative is that we cannot draw a line through ourselves and thus separate our imbalance from our self. We cannot selectively decide which parts of our core self we want to be and which parts we refuse. Our imbalance *is* an essential part of us. To eradicate our imbalance would be akin to plucking our eyes from our head. It was given to us as a gift, to serve us so that we may serve others. Consider the following story:

Death of a Dream

I recently got an emergency call from a man whose friends took him to the hospital when they determined he was delusional. He said he was up all night, inundated with visions that brought past and future crashing together in the now. "It was one hundred times more than I normally handle," he said. The hospital staff wanted to medicate him to quiet the voices, which he was afraid would cut him off in the middle of what he considered a spiritual experience.

Sixteen years ago, he had a powerful vision of how he was intended to walk his Lifepath and serve the people around him. Nobody understood, and before the year was out, he was diagnosed with bipolar disorder. His psychiatrist labeled his periodic guiding revelations, which normally follow a visionary experience, as "psychotic episodes" and drugged him down to the point where he could maintain a job and a relationship. The "episodes" stopped, only at a cost—his spiritual experiences stopped as well. He was diagnosed with cancer of the spleen and a 40 percent loss of kidney function from having to continually process the medications "treating" his bipolar "disorder."

In a Native culture, this man would have been held in esteem as a seer, a soul journeyer. His people would have looked forward to the healings and prophetic visions coming from his mystic excursions. The Elders would have guided him, the men would have assured his safety, and the women would have provided for his comfort. Nothing about the experience or its offerings would have been considered disordered or disorderly.

Doing It Differently

In *The Tangled Wing: Biological Constraints on the Human Spirit*, Melvin Konner writes that "Depression, delusion, obsession, compulsion, overeating, addiction, and attention deficit are all treated with medicines. Yet one need only change this list to read sadness, imagination, conscientiousness, diligence, appetite, habit, and restlessness to realize how very close we are to managing human nature by prescription."[8]

What is labeled an *illness* or *imbalance* could instead be an unexpressed or unmet need. Or it might be a unique way to meet a need in my community and bring Balance to my Relations. The ego's lines of separation determine mental imbalance as isolated to the individual, without looking at the individual as part of her or his clan. Just as the human body maintains homeostasis and a physical sense of balance, the human community maintains harmony and balance through our diversity—for instance, it is not necessary for *everyone* to be a Guardian, Nurturer, and Voice all at once. Our culture has overemphasized the concept of balance within us at the expense of the balance between us.

Instead of seeking this balance, our culture has prioritized normalcy and has pathologized as "illness" anything that makes us distinct—the very things that would help bring balance at the level of the community. I wonder how many people with alleged psychological conditions are actually gifted in ways that do not fit with contemporary life or beliefs. I dream about how rich and centered life could be if we had these people's guiding voices.

I regularly come across misdiagnoses by mental health professionals. They prescribe counseling and medication regimens for people who often have needs that are entirely unrelated to the therapy profession, not to mention those who have no needs at all. My concern is about the misdiagnoses and not the mental health professionals who are doing the misdiagnosing. Most of them I know are dedicated and caring individuals doing the best they can with the training they've been given. The issue is much greater than any individual, or even the mental health profession—it lies in the cultural beliefs about mental illness that have given rise to that profession.

Common Misdiagnoses

We now take a look at three common sets of misdiagnoses that are related to:

1. Attention, personality, or stress
2. Hormonal imbalances or nutritional deficiencies
3. Lifestyle

First on the list of misdiagnoses is the group of mental disorders headlined by Attention Deficit Disorder/Attention Deficit Hyperactivity Disorder (ADD/ADHD), Dissociative Identity Disorder (DID), and Post-Traumatic Stress Disorder (PTSD). Considering the controversy surrounding the very existence of these conditions,[9,]

[10, 11] labeling people with the term *disorder* should be considered a discriminatory act.

Attention-based "disorders" are especially marketed as objective diagnoses, even though this labeling has historically changed based on cultural pressures and needs.[12] Researchers have also made the case that differences in rates of ADHD globally point to the role of culture in creating, diagnosing, and understanding the "illness."[13]

Meanwhile, in the case of DID, there is even doubt over whether symptoms exist and what they may be.[14, 15, 16, 17] As for PTSD, the criteria for a diagnosis have become progressively broader since the American Psychiatric Association first listed it as a mental disorder in 1980.[18] The concept has also been criticized within the field of psychiatry as harmful to patients and damaging to our understanding of natural human responses to trauma.[19] For an exploration of the validity of PTSD as a diagnosis, please see my book *Wilderness Stress and Trauma*.

In an interview with PBS, Harvard-educated psychiatrist Peter Breggin described the example of Snowball, "a caged animal, a polar bear, in the [Calgary] zoo in Toronto, who was pacing up and down and looking uncomfortable, and looking like he'd really like to go back to the Arctic ... And they put him on Prozac, and he stopped pacing ... He sat quietly and looked happy. And animal rights people gathered to the zoo and protested the drugging of a polar bear to make him into a good caged animal, and he was taken off the drug."[20, 21]

We diagnose and medicate each other in order to better fit into and endure a diseased culture. Perhaps scarier than our culture placing us in mental cages is when we're made to feel comfortable there. As with the three so-called disorders listed above, we pathologize behaviors that we find disruptive—without regard for what underlying needs those behaviors might point to, or even what assets these behaviors might be for our community. Since these "illnesses" rest on subjective values and interpretations of life experiences, what we consider a disorder in our culture may be considered an asset in another.

This second category of misdiagnoses affects people who have hormonal imbalances or nutritional deficiencies. They can get diagnosed with anything from depression to dementia, when what they really need is an appointment with a holistic physician for a physical exam and blood work. A prime example is a woman I went to school with who struggled through her school years with depression and lack of energy. Finally, it dawned on someone to check her hormone levels. After her third kidney was removed, she instantly transformed into an effervescent woman with boundless energy. I know another woman who was seeing a counselor for three years due to her continual struggle with depression. Eventually she went to a holistic MD and found out that she had a severe Vitamin D deficiency.

The third category is lifestyle-related. Poor diet, substance abuse, obesity, and lack of exercise can either cause or contribute to numerous psycho-emotional imbalances, as well as the appearance of imbalances. Take a man I know who was depressed and suicidal. His marriage fell apart, and the endless weekly counseling sessions only added to the feeling that his life was at a dead end. Then a couple of his friends who were active outdoors people started dragging him along on canoe trips and snowshoeing outings, and within a few months, you would hardly know he was the same person. He moved out into the country, got a new job, started dating, and he now initiates activities rather than having to be dragged along.

My suggestions for a solution:

- Have all prospective mental health patients receive a lifestyle assessment and a complete physical exam by a holistic MD.

- Expand the practice of psychotherapy to include lifestyle and nutritional elements. It's not about getting rid of psychotherapy; it's about focusing less on finding an *illness* and instead turning our attention to our core natures, ways of living, and roles in our communities.

- Reassess all individuals diagnosed with DID, PTSD, ADD/ADHD with the goal of preparing the vast majority of them to lead lives in resonance with their special innate talents and gifts and undoing the damage from trying to make them into something they are not intended to be.

The Role of Perspective

Wellness is a state of being. Psychological trauma or chemical imbalances in the brain may have very real effects on our lives, though part of our *illness* lies in thinking we are sick. When we think we are sick, we stop recognizing what is whole and healed in us. If we think we are dying, we are dying. If we think we are living, we are living.

There probably will never come a time when any of us are completely healed—yet that does not mean we are forever broken. The more we heal, the more the world opens up to us, and the more we realize there is still something to learn. When we climb our first mountain, we stand at the summit and look to a new horizon. We quickly realize that ours is not the only mountain. Countless peaks lay before us. Do we give up in despair since it took so much energy and so much of our lifetime to climb this mountain, or do we give thanks for the teachings of the journey and rejoice in all the teaching gifts that lie before us as we climb the next mountain and the next?

If there were a boundary at which point we transition from being unhealed to healed, that would imply that one day we can stop healing—which would be as counterintuitive and harmful as expecting to reach the point when I have eaten enough food and don't have to eat anymore. The gifts of healing do not lie at *the end*—they are cumulative and come only with walking every step of the path of our healing.

This is why life is referred to as a Path. It was never intended that we find a particular place on our Path, then sit there. If we are not willing to give of ourselves, to put the effort into the walking, we do not progress on our Path. And remember, we are all walking the Path *together*—the notion of separation is only an illusion, which means that there is still healing to be done as long as there is woundedness and heartache in the world. When we reach one of the many peaks of our own healing journey, it is incumbent on us to turn our attention to others on the Path and offer our support.

Chapter in a Page

Jiddu Krishnamurti said, "It is no measure of health to be well adjusted to a profoundly sick society." Our culture labels people's eccentricities, talents, and even core emotions as signs of *illness* and *disease*. "Mental illness" is distinct from a physical injury, anatomical abnormality, or deterioration of the brain due to a pathogen. It is largely a myth.

The concept is anchored to our belief in objectivity. Subjective experience is considered *delusional* or *disordered* in relation to "objective" reality. This belief is persistent even though many diagnoses have changed or even disappeared with cultural shifts.

Our biases stem from the ego and the dichotomous mind, which draw lines of separation. These lines split the *self* from the *other* and trap us on either side of a right-wrong, good-bad binary between life and death, justice and injustice, sickness and wellness, and so on. This defines our mental imbalances as a sickness, yet the truth is we cannot separate our imbalance from our self; we can't select parts of our core self and disown the rest. Imbalance *is* irrevocably a part of us. It is a gift that helps us serve others.

The status quo also isolates the individual from her clan when making a mental illness diagnosis. A so-called illness could point to an unmet need of an individual or a community. Our contemporary health professionals tend to emphasize the balance within us at the expense of the balance between us. How many people with alleged psychological conditions are actually gifted? Think how rich life could be if we had these people's guiding voices.

We can expand the practice of psychotherapy to include lifestyle and nutritional elements. When we focus on our core natures, special innate talents, ways of living, and roles in our communities, we can recognize wellness as a state of being. When we think we are sick, we stop recognizing what is whole and healed in us.

8: We Believe in Mental Illness Endnotes

1   It appears that the quote is from a speech as it does not appear in any text search; the following three sources are books that each use the quote and attribute it to Jiddu Krishnamurti, so there is precedent:

Blake Bauer, "Love Your Body, But Know You Are So Much More," in *You Were Not Born to Suffer: Love Yourself Back to Inner Peace, Health, Happiness, & Fulfillment* (Bloomington, IN: Balboa, 2012), 151.

Frank Lipman and Mollie Doyle, "Prepare," in *Revive: Stop Feeling Spent and Start Living Again* (New York, NY: Pocket Books, 2009), 38.

John Maxwell Taylor, "Conspirituality—A Gathering Storm of Consciousness or the Aquarian Conspiracy Gone Wrong?" in *The Enlightenment Quest and the Art of Happiness: Mastering Life through Higher Power* (Berkeley, CA: North Atlantic, 2015), 94.

2   Thomas Szasz, "The Myth of Mental Illness," *American Psychologist* 15, no. 2 (1960): 113-18.

3   Ibid.

4   Cecilia Tasca, et al., "Women and Hysteria in the History of Mental Health," *Clinical Practice and Epidemiology in Mental Health: CP & EMH* 8 (2012): 110.

5   Kathleen Ritter and Anthony I. Terndrup. "Concepts of Sexual Orientation." *Handbook of Affirmative Psychotherapy with Lesbians and Gay Men* (New York: Guilford, 2002), 25-46.

6   Lisa Keen and Suzanne B. Goldberg, "The Science of Sexuality," in *Strangers to the Law: Gay People on Trial* (Ann Arbor: U of Michigan, 1998), 43-74.

7   Nancy Bearss, "Working With Lesbian, Gay, Bisexual, and Transgender Youth in Schools," in *Handbook of Culturally Responsive School Mental Health: Advancing Research, Training, Practice, and Policy* (New York: Springer, 2013), 89-105.

8 Melvin Konner, *The Tangled Wing: Biological Constraints on the Human Spirit* (New York: Holt, 2003), xix-xx.

9 Keith McBurnett and Linda Pfiffner, *Attention Deficit Hyperactivity Disorder: Concepts, Controversies, New Directions* (CRC Press, 2007), 323.

10 Paulette Marie Gillig, "Dissociative Identity Disorder: A Controversial Diagnosis," *Psychiatry (Edgmont)* 6, no. 3 (2009): 24.

11 Paul R. McHugh and Glenn Treisman, "PTSD: A Problematic Diagnostic Category," *Journal of Anxiety Disorders* 21, no. 2 (2007): 211-22.

12 Rick Mayes and Adam Rafalovich, "Suffer the Restless Children: The Evolution of ADHD and Paediatric Stimulant Use, 1900–80," *History of Psychiatry* 18, no. 4 (2007): 435-57.

13 Sami Timimi and Eric Taylor, "ADHD is Best Understood As A Cultural Construct," *The British Journal of Psychiatry* 184, no. 1 (2004): 8-9.

14 Arnold Lieber, "Multiple Personality Disorder (Dissociative Identity Disorder)," *PSYCOM*, last modified March 2009, accessed October 2020, https://www.psycom.net/mchugh.html.

15 NP Spanos, "Hypnosis, Nonvolitional Responding, and Multiple Personality: A Social Psychological Perspective," *Prog. Exp. Pers. Res.* 14, no. 1 (1986): 62.

16 HS Decker, JM Quen, "The Lure of Non-Materialism in Materialist Europe: Investigations of Dissocative Phenomenon," *Split Minds/Split Brains: Historical and Current Perspectives* (New York: NYU Press; 1986), 31-62.

17 Paulette Marie Gillig, "Dissociative Identity Disorder: A Controversial Diagnosis," *Psychiatry (Edgmont)* 6, no. 3 (2009): 24.

18 Mary E. Long and Jon D. Elhai. "Posttraumatic Stress Disorder's Traumatic Stressor Criterion: History, Controversy, and Clinical and Legal Implications," *Psychological Injury and Law* 2, no. 2 (2009): 167-78.

19 Paul R. McHugh and Glenn Treisman, "PTSD: A Problematic Diagnostic Category," *Journal of Anxiety Disorders* 21, no. 2 (2007): 211-22.

20 "Interview: Peter Breggin," *Frontline*, last modified 3 May 2000, accessed 22 July 2015, http://www.pbs.org/wgbh/pages/frontline/shows/medicating/interviews/breggin.html.

21 "Calgary Zoo Makes Room for Polar Bears, Pandas in New Plan," *CBCnews*. CBC/Radio Canada, last modified 26 April 2013, accessed 22 July 2015, http://www.cbc.ca/news/canada/calgary/calgary-zoo-makes-room-for-polar-bears-pandas-in-new-plan-1.1346630.

9: We Tell Ourselves We Are Depressed

The White Mountain Apache tell about the long-ago time when their tribe, along with the wild animals and birds, lived together near white people. Coyote, who was always getting in trouble, visited among the camps, staying in one for a while, then moving on. When he stayed at Bear's camp, he would go at night to the white man's fields and steal wheat.

When the white man who owned the farm found out what Coyote was up to, he trailed him long enough to locate his path into the field. Then he called all the white men to a council, and they made a figure of pitch just like a man and placed it in Coyote's path.

That night when Coyote went back to steal wheat again, he saw the pitch man standing there. Thinking it was a real person, he said, "Gray eyes, get to one side and let me by. I just want a little wheat. Get over, I tell you."

The pitch man stayed where he was.

"If you don't move," Coyote said, "you'll get my fist in your face. Wherever I go on this earth, if I hit a man with my fist, it kills him."

The pitch man never stirred.

"All right, then I'm going to hit you."

Coyote struck out, and his fist stuck fast in the pitch, clear to his elbow.

"What's the matter?" Coyote cried. "Why have you caught my hand? Turn loose or you'll get my other fist. If I hit a man with that one, it knocks all his wits out!"

Then Coyote punched with his other fist, and that arm got stuck in the pitch also. Now he was standing on his two hind legs.

"I'm going to kick you if you keep holding me, and it'll knock you over."

Coyote delivered a powerful kick, and his leg went into the pitch and stuck.

This other leg is worse still, and you're going to get it!" he said.

He kicked, and his leg stuck into the pitch. Now only his tail was free.

"If I whip you with my tail, it will cut you in two. So turn me loose!"

The pitch man just stood there. Coyote lashed the pitch with his tail, and it stuck also.

"Why do you hold me this way?" snarled Coyote. "I'll bite you in the neck and kill you, so you'd better turn me loose!"

When the pitch man did nothing, Coyote bit it and got his mouth stuck, and there he was.

In the morning, the farmer put a chain around Coyote's neck, took him out of the pitch, and led him to the house. "This is the one who has been stealing from me," he said to his family. The white people held a meeting to discuss what they should do with Coyote. They decided to scald him in a pot of boiling water.

Wilfred Pelletier, a Canadian Odawa, said that our contemporary culture is dependent on an *enemy concept*: "For everything you do, you must end up fighting—fighting for your rights, good against evil, war against poverty, the fight for peace. The whole base of the western culture has an enemy concept. What would happen if you remove the enemy? How then do you defeat somebody who is on your side? I suspect that if you remove the enemy, the culture might collapse."

Much like Coyote, we are led by our culture's concept of mental illness to battle against pitch men—we make up enemies where there are none. Consider one of the biggest pitch men of our culture these days: depression as a mental illness. The intense sadness that we associate with depression is real and is felt. The question is not about the feelings per se, it's what we have made them into—just as in the Apache legend, the question is not whether or not there is a pitch man in the road, it's what Coyote makes of that figure.

Depression is not a malevolent foe: It is nothing more and nothing less than an expression of our core emotion of sadness. By transforming it into an *illness* and thinking we must *fight* it, we are no better than Coyote—our effort and our courage are noble, yet the fight itself is misguided and counterintuitive: With every swipe, we are left more stuck and feeling more helpless.

The pitch man is not Coyote's enemy; in fact, the pitch man could have been an ally, as he is a warning to Coyote that the farmer is seeking his capture. Yet as Coyote fights the pitch man, this truth of the moment is left unheard. When we are able to embrace depression for what it is instead of fighting what it is not, we can listen to what the emotion is telling us. This perspective allows us to move beyond the enemy concept and stop fighting, which is not the same as giving up: It is remembering that we are walking the Path of Life together and when we stop externalizing and blaming, we give ourselves a chance to heal.

Depression's Identity Revealed

We use the term *depression* freely, as if there were a single understanding of the term—yet there isn't. Depression is used as a literal and a metaphorical term. The term describes an individual abnormality, a cultural normality, a temporary reaction, a longstanding condition, an intangible emotional state, and a biological condition. It is treated as synonymous with sadness, guilt, and lack of motivation, as well as a combination of these. It is everything, and it is nothing.

Depression is not a discovery in the sense of, say, discovering a vaccine for polio or a new species; depression is a construction, a category that we use to describe people. Categories can be helpful, as long as they are accurate. However, psychiatric classifications in general, and depression in particular, have been described as having *weak construct validity*—meaning that psychiatric tests are not very good at measuring the things they claim to be measuring, such as whether or not a person has depression. Depression has long been difficult to distinguish from sadness, grief, guilt, or simply having a low mood.

Many of the "symptoms" that accompany a diagnosis of depression—lack of sleep, poor concentration, self-criticism, guilt, thoughts of death—are also aspects of unhappiness or sadness. In other words: real human feelings, not signs of illness. This symptomology and the notion of depression as an illness are highly cultural. Our culture medicalizes the individual, while other cultures look at circumstances, morals, or community-level factors. The way Western societies treat depression—through individualized, chemical, and private efforts—is directly attributable to the perception of depression as an individual illness.

We cannot ignore that there is money to be made with this perspective, namely for the drug companies that produce and market antidepressants. These companies influence the way doctors prescribe medication—so much so that it has been said that we face an epidemic of depression prescriptions more so than an epidemic of depression., , It has even been shown that depression is overdiagnosed: In one study, more than a quarter of non-depressed patients were diagnosed as clinically depressed. There is also research suggesting that some elderly individuals are diagnosed with depressive disorders when their symptoms may be factors of normal aging. What's more, the effect of chemical antidepressants has more often than not been weaker than the placebo effect.

Depression as an illness is at the forefront of a cultural mentality in which we are led to believe we cannot know ourselves without the intermediary of diagnostic tests, objective observers, and pharmaceutical drugs. We made a supposedly rational decision that we must prescribe and medicalize everyday life. We're told we should want to be symptom-free, yet when the symptoms are really our emotions, we're ultimately striving for an unfeeling life. Our goal, as psychotherapist Gary Greenberg has noted, is *antidepression*, not happiness. To seek relief, we turn to drugs and psychotherapy, although seldom is a cure effected. Usually we feel blessed if we can become more functional, less suicidal. We soothe the bruise while at the same time we keep getting bruised.

Think of treating depression with talk therapy as an editor trying to correct the grammar of an abstract watercolor painting. She can ply her dictionary, red pencil, and creative writing degree, yet she still finds herself staring only at a painting. She might talk with the artist about what brought him to write this unreadable piece and how his fortunes could turn if he used more intelligible words, and he might play along. Still, it means nothing to him, as there are no words of any sort or form embedded in that painting.

Think of depression as a lack of feeling and motivation—nothing to describe with words. The editor would likely see that if she were to set aside her tools and training and quit trying to extract—or invent—words from the intangible. If instead she would just *be* with the artist in wordlessness, she might find empathy with him.

Depression, as many of us know it (the debilitating, life-altering form), is not intrinsic to being Human. For many, depression is cyclical in nature; for some, it is omnipresent. Whatever the case and however mild or oppressive, it exists to raise awareness and offer guidance. It is not an illness as much as it is a symptom of a deeper imbalance. So treating it as one would treat an illness pacifies the symptom without knowing or honoring the cause. We go on, numb to its presence and unaware of its intended wisdom for us.

Some of us may confuse our innate sadness, especially when we feel it strongly, with depression. Clinical depression is often the result of neglect of the anxiety underlying unresolved fear, anger, or longing, which is a symptom of imbalance within our Heart-of-Hearts.

When we honor these feelings and the anxiety that accompanies them, we do not come down with depression. Remember, our core emotions are part of our core self—feeling them, even feeling them strongly, does not make us sick; it makes us human.

How Depression Serves Us

Depression is a survival mechanism, intended to be temporary. However, since victimization is endemic to our culture, so also is depression. It then becomes the chronic state of being for a great number of people. Some describe it as though it were a blanket of snow covering everything. They know there is life under the snow that is hibernating; it is muffled under this heavy, dark blanket that numbs everything and makes it feel inaccessible, far away. The blanket makes them feel they can no longer affect the means and ends of their existence, so they begin to shut down and deny that existence.

All creatures are designed for one essential purpose—to be active players in life. When that is not a viable option, life itself is denied that individual. Depression becomes his coping mechanism; he disengages from life and retreats from it to the point where he is no longer being actively victimized. He goes on subsisting in this dulled and diminished state until either his situation changes or his life ends. This is just one story of depression. It doesn't have to be the only one.

Charles Darwin wrote in 1887 that "Pain or suffering of any kind, if long continued, causes depression and lessens the power of action; yet it is well adapted to make a creature guard itself against any great or sudden evil." Things that we regard as debilitating, unpleasant, and sad do serve a purpose—for instance, an infant's crying may signal to its parents that it is hungry or in pain.,

Depression may serve as an indication that one's relationships, priorities, commitments, and actions need to change, as they may be unattainable, unfulfilling, or harmful., , Our emotions do not occur in a vacuum. They manifest in response to our experiences and provide insight into how we should proceed—they help us manage and navigate distinct life situations to our advantage., , , , , The emotional experience is an asset. If we are feeling depressed, that feeling is manifesting for a reason—something is not functioning in our life and we need to address it. When we treat our emotions as symptoms of an illness, then we cut off access to this wisdom.

Perhaps we can best honor depression by first welcoming it. With acceptance of depression as having a place within us and even being *of* us rather than establishing an *it vs. me* relationship, we allow ourselves the potential for new perspective and teaching. We also help reduce distress around it.

Everything has its reason. If we don't understand it at first, that's okay. Sometimes if we can connect with the same feeling we've had in the past, we can at least connect with where it's coming from. When we identify its source, sometimes we can do something about it. In that way, we may not fully grasp the feeling in this moment, yet we can perhaps notice the continuum of that feeling. The important thing is that we remember to embrace it without being victimized. When we see our feeling as an illness or a pathogen, it's much harder to not feel attacked by it. It's when we see our feeling as our guide that we don't need to run away.

It can be intimidating at first to sit with your feelings of depression—to allow yourself to just be with it, experience the sadness fully. If you can do that, though, then you are honoring it for what it is; you're letting yourself viscerally explore the sadness, even though you don't consciously identify it, where it came from or what's causing it. If you're allowing yourself to just feel it, it works itself out. Maybe it starts feeling familiar to you; maybe you connect it with something. Maybe your visions of the past come forth, and they provide insight into the way you're feeling.

Embracing the feeling can be an active process that involves asking ourselves open-ended questions, such as:

- What is the function of my depression?
- What is its voice, and how can I understand it?
- Why does it visit at particular times?

The answers to these questions are probably different for each of us. They can be found with the help of our dreams, our intuitive voice, and from the Circle Consciousness. A personal guide who is versed in such matters could also be helpful.

Depression can also serve us when we rethink the context in which we experience it. In our culture, depression is considered a problem of the individual. Healing involves moving beyond this isolating paradigm that also feeds into the enemy concept. To consider depression as my problem alone makes it difficult to open up, to approach others, and to ask for help. To experience sadness or disengagement to the fullest, you may need to experience it in the context of others. This may mean honoring your need to cry—and instead of crying alone in the corner, imagine what it would be like to cry in somebody's empathetic arms. Someone who's there to listen and support you and keep you connected. And that someone isn't always a human—it might be a tree, or even the wind. It's all about staying engaged with the feeling, your core self, and your Relations.

Mental health is relevant every day for every person; we need to take personal responsibility for our well-being and that of those close to us. In the Circle Way, we are responsible to each other. I am aware of my neighbor, and my neighbor is aware of me, and we are actively engaged in each other's wellness. We are parenting each other. The parent doesn't approach the infant only when she cries; the parent is proactively invested in connecting to her wellness.

Depression Is Part of Balance

In life we naturally expand and contract, open and close, in the same rhythm as our breathing. When we remain closed, that is when depression sets in.

A few days ago, someone who struggles with on-and-off chronic depression called me. He told me about the meditation he practiced every morning to help him begin his day feeling centered and at peace. He said it was working well. In fact, that morning he was overcome with tears of joy. However, it didn't last. That afternoon, when he called, tears were flowing for another reason; he was overcome with anxiety and confusion. He asked me how that could be—how he could start the day so energized, then a few short hours later, sink into the depths of depression. I explained to him Balance as I knew it. That being in a state of Balance is not dwelling in a steady, unchanging, stable emotional climate. Rather it is a cycle, just as the cycle of the Seasons and the cycle of day and night. It is the yin and yang of things. The farther the pendulum is pushed one way, the farther it swings the other way. That is the way of Balance.

If I strive for an emotional high, I would do well to expect an emotional low to follow it, to balance it out. The energy for the high has to come from somewhere, and if we are to have another high, that energy needs to be recharged. We also need the downtime to integrate the blessings and teachings of the high and to prepare for the next one. This is exemplified noticeably in creative People, many of whom have wildly productive periods full of inspiration and good energy flow before they crash.

A crash can initiate a brooding, introspective time, accompanied by a contrary, challenging, questioning energy. Old assumptions are undermined, old work is critiqued, and old approaches lose their appeal. Nothing seems to satisfy. If creative output is attempted during this time, it only leads to frustration and lack of productivity, for the failed effort can easily undermine self-esteem.

Those who do not understand this creative cycle sometimes label it as depression and encourage treatment or medication. Sometimes the creative Person buys into the assessment and self-medicates. Both scenarios are rare when the creative Person is understood and supported—when her "depression" is seen for what it is: part of the ebb and flow of personal energy.-

Unfortunately, many of us do not understand our own rhythms, so when we're feeling down, we think there is something wrong, something out of kilter. We want to feel good; we want to feel up. We either self-medicate or find a specialist to medicate us. This begins the treadmill—an unending spiral of artificial highs followed by equally dramatic lows. Before long, we find that we have become addicted to our fix. To maintain balance, we need to continually ingest antidepressants, anxiety medications, or stimulants. If we self-medicate, we find ourselves continually ingesting starch, sugar, caffeine, chocolate, dairy, movies, meditation, novels, gossip—whatever we have found to keep us from knowing and experiencing the true cycle of our energy and our feelings.

What has happened is that we have become afraid of ourselves— we live in fear of who we are without our addiction. We are like a bird who can't really fly, so she lives with the illusion of flying by suspending herself in the air with a string tied to a branch. Our depression epidemic is really an epidemic of people who do not know themselves. Along with that, the epidemic is an indictment of a culture that no longer understands the natural Balance of the individual, so it can no longer support the natural rhythms of Balance. It has become a culture of illusion, trying to create a society of stable individuals who are always the same—always bright, gregarious, and outgoing. And let's not forget, always productive.

Maintaining Balance

Exercise is a sustainable and cost-effective alternative to chemical antidepressants or psychotherapy. Physical exercise reduces symptoms of depression, and this effect appears to be long-lasting., A meta-analysis of fifty-eight studies of the relationship between exercise and depression concluded that exercise treatments resulted in lower scores of depression compared to control treatments. Meanwhile, running specifically has been shown to be equally as effective as psychotherapy in reducing symptoms of depression.

Not all of us, though, whether due to injury or difference in ability, are able to incorporate significant exercise or running routines into our lives. One of the most effective techniques I have found for restoring Balance to my life, and maintaining it, is to be conscious about my sleep patterns.

Sleep is critical for leading a mentally balanced life. Disrupted sleep or misaligned circadian rhythms are commonly present in people diagnosed with psychiatric disorders. One reason I go to bed early in the evening is that this rhythm is more conducive to peaceful, rejuvenating sleep than late-night rhythms. It turns out that the old saying, *An hour of sleep before midnight is worth two after,* holds some truth regarding the quality of sleep. Deep, restorative sleep occurs during the first third of the night, which is typically before and around midnight. Sleep later in the night is more easily disturbed.

Research has also found that going to sleep after fighting or arguing is significantly correlated with greater sleep disruption. If there is strife between my mate and me, we make peace before falling asleep so that we can greet sleep calmly. I don't read before sleeping, as the transition between my awake world and my dream world is a special, sacred time of day, deserving of the cleansing and contemplation befitting the entry of one world from another.

I also heed the wisdom of my Elders to be up with the Sun. He is our father, with gifts of warmth and light. Those who habitually arise at dawn begin their days infused with His energy. They have an emotional edge that makes them less prone to depression. Morning energy is so strong that it even touches those who sleep in, as they cannot rest as well as in the night.   When we sleep in, we shun Sun's gifts and dishonor His fathership. Virtually all of our plant and animal relations rise with the Sun; when we sleep in, we lose out on sharing the joy of starting a new day and honoring Sun Father with them. We are then out of sync with them, and thereby out of sync with ourselves, as they are us and we are them. Late-risers fare no better later in the day. Research into the relationship between a person's circadian rhythm and personality has confirmed that there is a positive correlation between morningness, or being a morning person, and mental stability. In a separate study, the quality of eveningness, or being an evening person, was associated with higher levels of depression.

Getting up at dawn is not just a physical practice we can cultivate; it is also a metaphor for our approach to healing. It represents being conscious, present, and engaged all the time. And not just with your circle—with yourself as well. When we rise with the sun, we rise in alignment with the day and with ourselves. When we are present with the day and present in ourselves, we are in the precise state of being that nurtures wellness.

Chapter in a Page

Depression is not a disease—it's a category we use to describe people. Moreover, many psychiatric classifications, particularly depression, *have weak construct validity*, meaning they don't accurately measure the things they claim to be measuring.

Depression is seldom distinguished from sadness, grief, guilt, or simply having a low mood. Our Western culture also isolates and medicalizes the individual instead of looking to circumstances, morals, or community-level causes. Treatment typically follows financial incentives, so it's unsurprising that depression is overdiagnosed and chemical antidepressants rarely perform better than the placebo effect.

We can embrace and honor depression without becoming its victim. Remember, everything has a reason—even debilitating, unpleasant, and sad things serve a purpose. Start by welcoming the emotion. When we accept depression and eschew *it vs. me* thinking, we open ourselves to a new perspective. We also reduce our distress about it.

Depression is a natural response to certain experiences, and it guides action. It's not an illness as much as a signifier of a deeper imbalance. It may indicate that our relationships, priorities, commitments, and actions must change, as they may be unattainable, unfulfilling, or harmful. Treating it like an illness pacifies the symptom without honoring the cause. We remain unaware of its intended wisdom.

Healing involves moving beyond our isolating, individualistic cultural paradigm. We may need to open up, approach others, and ask for help. To experience sadness or disengagement to the fullest, you may need to experience it with others. Find someone who's there to listen and support you and keep you connected. That someone isn't always a human. The point is to stay engaged with the feeling, your core self, and your Relations.

Mental health is an everyday affair, and in the Circle Way, we are responsible to each other. We are parenting each other. A parent is proactively invested in the wellness of the infant, not just when he cries.

10: We Keep Relying on Talk Therapy

We have a popular conception of talk therapy, also commonly known as *psychotherapy*, *psychoanalysis*, or simply *counseling*, as a contemporary phenomenon originating with Sigmund Freud in the nineteenth and early twentieth centuries. It actually has its roots in ancient Greece. Diogenes of Sinope, whom we discussed in *#3*, espoused the Greek philosophy of Cynicism, which sought full mental lucidity as its goal. This school of thought later influenced the Greek philosophy of Stoicism that is credited as the original template for contemporary models of counseling.[1] Stoicism's practitioners considered philosophy a method in the art of living—a way to manage the concerns of everyday life with tranquility. Back then, the philosophers and physicians were the counselors, yet the approach was the same as now—therapy based on a sequence of issue-based talk sessions.

Whatever the era and whatever the school of practice (more than 500 to date), talk therapy is based on the core assumptions that:

1. We can schedule our healing in a periodic fashion.
2. We can heal ourselves by repeatedly verbalizing an issue.
3. We can depend on a counselor to guide, or at least manage, this verbalization.

These assumptions can be boiled down to a belief that our healing is verbal, intermittent, and in the hands of someone other than ourselves.

Most of us see our therapists week after week, month after month, and sometimes year after year. After our initial session cycle is terminated, we often find ourselves starting a new one. Yet many of us prematurely discontinue our session cycle, even after switching to a new counselor. A 2012 meta-analysis of 669 studies of psychotherapy dropout concluded that one in five clients discontinue treatment without finishing it.[2] Attrition from talk therapy is on par with what it was half a century ago.[3] According to the American Psychological Association, the rate of client dropout for some counselors reaches up to 75 percent.[4]

The failure rate has spawned a flurry of activity throughout the past two decades to discover more effective alternatives. Having worked professionally with twenty-plus psychotherapists in recent years, along with my client counseling work and personal history with counselors, I've been able to assess the efficacy of the talk therapy approach firsthand. I called my counselor desperately a few times when I didn't think I could make it to my next weekly appointment. I kept going to counselors for years before I got fed up with my dependence on endless weekly visits and decided to start taking personal responsibility for my life. My experiences and those of others I know have led me to conclude that the fundamental healing many of us crave can be inhibited by endless weekly visits to the therapist and an unending parade of healing modalities.

It takes two things to heal—courage and embracing our fear. Good therapists can help us find both. At the same time, approaching talk therapy as a consumer commodity can keep us from finding both within ourselves. This is a critically important point in our healing, as anything less than both just prolongs our misery and codependence. Many of us end up substituting a codependent intimate relationship with a codependent relationship with a counselor or healing technique. In this chapter, we discuss how to move in the opposite direction. We explore the areas where talk therapy lets us down and what we can do about it.

Where Talk Therapy Fails

In our culture, we like to believe that we can segment our lives—that just as we go to the gym to strengthen our bodies, we can schedule in a discrete amount of time for our psycho-emotional tuning. A visit to the therapist is just another errand to pencil in.

Traditional cultures did not have this separated mode of life, so they had no need for modern counseling, which is built on the premise that people today are isolated and didn't have the opportunity to form secure attachments growing up. In a tribe, this context would never arise, and so it would never be an issue. Sadly, in our culture, sometimes the best option people can find is a once-a-week nurturing relationship with a medical professional.

These brief and routinized talk therapy sessions keep us functional, yet disempowered. Before we've even begun talking, our healing is weighed down by budget, insurance, and scheduling constraints—both ours and the therapist's. A relationship that is intended to be about healing is always in the shadow of an economic transaction between a *client* and a *provider* rather than a Seeker and a Guide. We are then obliged to fit what we say into the allotted time of our appointment or pause and wait until the following week. Our healing is constantly in a process of starting and stopping, devoid of the sustained focus and attention it deserves in the moment.

Once upon a time, counseling was different. I would have gone to a Seer or Medicine Person, or I would have taken time to fast in the woods. And I would have been healed. I wouldn't just take a shower as I do now and rush to get to my appointment on time—which is usually squeezed between other appointments in a busy day. I would have prepared myself, perhaps by first petitioning the Healer, then fasting, along with crafting ritual objects to focus my contemplation. The healing itself would have been a profound event, usually involving those closest to me and marked by a feast or other ritual observance. Healing was a process that would have permeated my daily life and community rather than being a neatly bookended private conversation once a week. The Healer and the one to be healed would dwell together in a place of no boundaries, a place of complete trust with no eye on the clock.

Talking Our Way to Being Healed

The healing way of our ancestors and of Native people everywhere depends on direct communication in the language of the heart, upon core feelings, intuitive impressions, deep memories, and ancestral wisdom. The Healer can take many forms—a seer-shaman, a personal dodem (animal guide), the spirit of fire, a person's Dreamself, or a plant or animal helper. More important than the form of the Healer is the connection this figure has with the Dreamtime (a term derived from Australian Aboriginal traditions that we know variously as the *collective unconscious*, the *spirit world*, and the *astral plane*) and the ability to speak the language of the heart.

> **A WORD ABOUT THE DREAMTIME**
>
> The Australian Aborigines considered the Dreamtime a period when ancestral beings inhabited the earth and lived in unity with their natural Relations.[5] Connecting with the Dreamtime strengthens the threads that connect us with our ancestors, their wisdom, and their ways of being.

Talking is a counterproductive method for dealing with our core wound, which is rooted in our limbic mind. Words can't get us there, nor can they express it. Our ancestors understood that deep and lasting change must be effected nonverbally, in the limbic system where our long-term memories and core motivations dwell. When information enters the brain, it is directed either to the neocortex or the limbic process. Verbally based input goes to the neocortex, though it is the limbic process that is the seat of our consciousness and the location of our primary brain functioning. It also processes twenty or more times the input that the neocortex does. These two factors are what limit the scope and effectiveness of the talk therapy model, which privileges the rational mind over the limbic mind.

Since talk therapy is based on verbal language, it is reliant upon symbolic communication that transforms thoughts and feelings into words and phrases. Symbols need to be consciously chosen, which means that the mind needs to be involved. Talk therapy may invite the heart into the conversation, yet this communication is neither based in the heart nor an authentic reflection of it. Inevitably, as with all translations, something is lost in the process. Additionally, we must recognize that the symbolic medium is self-limiting, as it can convey only what can be rationally grasped. If anything, the conscious self may better serve the healing process by gracefully stepping aside and creating space for our intuition, our Dreamself, and our deep memories.

We experience and express many emotions nonverbally.[6] Although we are rational creatures with extensive language abilities, we do not verbalize all of our emotional experiences. Nonverbal communication is also essential to creating and maintaining close, intimate relationships with others.[7] Research has also shown that, in the case of experiences of love, there is a more or less equal balance between the verbal and nonverbal ways of communicating it.[8] As a result, people who are able to effectively decode and understand nonverbal cues are more likely to create and maintain intimate personal relationships.[9] Connection, growth, and healing often take place in a realm that is distinctly nonverbal.

How Repetition Creates Reality

In talk therapy, we run the risk of dwelling on the same story to the point that it can entrench and magnify trauma, dysfunctional behavior, and distorted views of reality. The more we talk about them, the greater the chance that they may become more deeply imprinted in our long-term memory. In essence, the more we dwell on them, the more they become our reality.

It doesn't matter whether our talk is positive or negative—and it doesn't even matter whether it's true or not. The mind does not distinguish between active and passive involvement or between speaking and listening. This is an evolved survival trait. When we live immersed in the means and ends of our existence, we cannot afford to distinguish between sources of information—everything must be given equal credence and attention.

Rethinking How We Counsel Others

We need to change how psychotherapeutic counselors see patients and also how they hear them. Psychoanalysis or talk therapy has transformed into a coercive form of dialogue in which the counselor molds the person-as-patient to fit society rather than giving the individual a chance to express her truths and have them embraced.[10] Success is seen as being able to function in the broken society that led the person to seek therapy. What was once a healing dialogue has become the search for an illness and, too often, the prescription of a cure.

When we look at the roots of the talk therapy model, we note that what made the ancient Greek approach work well is missing from the contemporary perspective. Ancient Greek medical practitioners looked at the ill person as a whole being rather than just a diseased body: Illness was a transformative and *personal* story.[11, 12] We, on the other hand, focus on the pathogen, the disease, or simply the idea of a disease, and treat the people affected as incidental (as in the example of the man diagnosed with bipolar disorder in #8).

Giving power back to the patient requires diverging partially from the ancient Greek model in which it was the job of the medical professional to tell the story of a person's illness and direct him toward healing.[13] It is my belief that we should be mindful of empowering the client, or Seeker, as I refer to them. Rather than providing healing and answers for the Seeker, the counselor helps guide him to finding the answers in himself.[14]

Academic programs produce technicians, not healers. They do tune-ups; we need to seek elsewhere to rest the crying of the soul. As I said in #8, the answer is not abandoning psychotherapy wholesale; it's changing the focus away from the search for an illness and toward our core natures, ways of living, and roles in our communities. As we do that, the role of the counselor naturally changes. Even though talk therapy is outmoded, there is still a place for counselors. They can serve a vital role in therapies that are geared toward action, with sessions used to map out healing strategies and assess results. Those counselors who are qualified could assume the role of Elders and mentors to guide us on our healing journeys.

Why Talk Therapy Remains Prevalent

There are three main reasons why—even though we recognize where it fails us—talk therapy remains entrenched in our culture:

1. **We see ourselves as primarily rational**, verbally oriented beings, thus concluding that our healing must also be rationally and verbally oriented.

2. **We have incorporated talk therapy into our economy**, which gives financial incentive to creating lengthy session contracts.

3. **We continually experience self-deception** and a lack of personal authenticity, and we (sometimes out of desperation) see talk therapy as our only hope.

The first two reasons have been discussed earlier in this chapter; it is the third that deserves attention here, as it is the main reason we can keep going to counselors for years and read self-help book after self-help book and still see no significant change. It's not so much that we don't know who we truly are as that we have created an illusion to take the place of our authentic self. We work so hard to create this illusion that we end up believing in it ourselves. And we have so much invested in our illusory self that we go to great pains to avoid or deny anything that would threaten the illusion. What we truly need is something that is not only going to rock our boat—it must sink it.

However, fear prevents us from going there on our own, and meanwhile, the system of talk therapy is not suited for cultivating authenticity. Authenticity is hard to talk about; it is a way of being. Pretense and illusion are also rooted in the neocortex, the same region of the brain that gives us speech, which is why we can talk about authenticity forever without moving from talking about it to living it. Enacted authenticity, on the other hand, is seated in the limbic region, the home of consciousness. There we do our deep thinking, which is not based on words—we walk it rather than talk it.

The Role of Deception

Let's take a look at why we create this illusory self in the first place. If living an illusion is so self-destructive and alienating, so undermining of our relationships, why do we do it? With the work I've done with people over the years as a teacher, guide, counselor, and researcher, I keep coming up with the same answer: Each of us finds ourselves alone in a sea of humanity.

In our culture, few of us have the security of strong, extended families (or clans, as with our early ancestors). We don't have the unconditionality of the close, loving relationships that those social structures gave us. And we don't practice personal quests for knowing self or rites of passage for evolving self, so we live in fear of being found out as just another lost and frightful individual.

We create what we consider to be a desirable and stable illusion for these basic reasons:

- To create a strong first impression

- To gain respect
- To avoid consequences
- To spare someone's feelings

We are often fully aware of the construction and maintenance of our illusory selves. Robert Feldman, a researcher at the University of Massachusetts, taped a series of ten-minute conversations and analyzed them to see how many times each person spun an illusion. It varied from person to person, and there was a slight gender difference, yet on average, each person gave three illusory statements within the ten-minute period. We each create about one hundred illusions on average per day.[15, 16] Is it any surprise, then, that we would start believing that we are what we've created?

We are hardwired to be self-deceived. For self-deception to occur, there must be two selves involved: the self that is doing the deceiving and the self that is being deceived.[17] Neurological research has found that some information can be accessed by certain parts of the brain and not others, creating a premise for the existence of these two selves.[18] We also know that human beings often act without fully knowing their motivations or what causes their behavior.[19, 20]

Deception is part of our natural development as human beings. Already at two to three years of age, we are manipulating our parents with illusions to avoid punishment or to get our needs met. And our parents encourage us to create illusions by urging us to say *thank you*, even if we don't like the present we were given, and to hug relatives or friends of our parents we hardly know. By the time we are four years of age, we project an illusion every two hours on average. By six years of age, it's down to every ninety minutes.[21] And it progresses from there until we are fully functioning adults, able to whip out illusory statements so efficiently that we average two to three lies during a typical ten-minute conversation.[22] We are all players in the game of self-deception and deception of others — even those of us who claim to create no illusions, as we generate *thirty times* more on average than those who admit to the practice.

My theory about why we resort to deception so early in our lives and so consistently is that it is a survival instinct gone awry. We are intrinsically hunters. For millions of years, we gained our sustenance by hunting and gathering, and the core of the hunt is deception. We have evolved an intuitive sense of secretiveness and creating illusions in order to effectively stalk an animal. When I disguise myself as Buffalo, I can get much closer to real Buffalo than if I approach them as my authentic self. Or if I create the illusion that I'm just passing by and have no interest in them, I can get within range to let my true feelings be known by unleashing an arrow. To survive, we need the nourishment gained from both food and friends, and apparently, we resort to the same techniques to secure both. Research in evolutionary social psychology also affirms that deception of others becomes easier, and appears more authentic, when we ourselves are deceived.[23, 24]

How to Live in Balance with Self-Deception

It is normal human behavior to deceive and be deceived. However, we harm ourselves when we take our deceptions (and the deceptions of others) seriously, and we harm our relationships when we use deception manipulatively. We lose touch with our authentic selves and undermine our connections with others.

To help us see through self-deception, we sometimes use satire. It may take the form of humor, irony, or plays on opposites. In some traditional cultures, special people play the role of satirists. They are known as contraries in the Plains American Indian cultures, and medieval courts had their jesters. Comedians play the role in our contemporary society, along with media venues such as comic strips, movies, and blogs. Since humor challenges the conventional, it allows us to take a step back from ourselves and our deceptions, to be self-critical in a nonaggressive way.

Here are some ways to guard against deception while still honoring our unique personal truths:

- Realize that each of us creates our own personal reality.
- Recognize that we each have our own truth.
- Avoid getting caught up in beliefs.
- Find humor in all things.
- Laugh at yourself.
- Seek constructive criticism.
- Take a daily dose of satire.

Reimagining Talk Therapy

To understand the current role of talk therapy in our mental health, let's use the metaphor of an old house. It's been passed down in the family for generations and has accumulated its share of dilapidation. The old outhouse and woodshed are still in the yard, though half-collapsed, while the yard itself is scraggly looking with an old car sitting out back from who-knows-when. In the back stands a newer shed built to accommodate long-forgotten objects from distant relatives.

Meanwhile, the house itself is a patchwork of added-on rooms and changed entryways. One busted-out window has plastic over it. The roof leaks, and the plumbing creaks. The porch is sagging, and the paint is peeling. It is an old, yet functional, house, and your family still lives there, just like your parents and their parents before them, somehow getting by from day to day and year to year. One day you decide to overhaul the house, so you hire an interior decorator, a handyperson, and a landscaper. After a week, you have new wallpaper, plush carpeting, and a renovated kitchen and bathroom. Outside, the house sparkles with a new paint job, a big deck with a barbeque grill and lounge chairs, and flowerbeds to brighten up the yard. The family is overjoyed, and you feel encouraged, as though you've got a new lease on life.

However, before long, the old grease stains start showing through the wallpaper, and the new cupboard doors don't shut right, thanks to the unstable wall the cupboard unit is mounted on. Winter comes, and cold drafts still find their way through the old walls, and on damp days, the mustiness from the basement still creeps into the house and irritates everybody's sinuses.

So you call the handyperson back to remount the cupboards and blow some insulation in the walls, and you ask the interior designer to put up a vinyl wallpaper that won't let the grease soak through. This cycle continues for years, and through the frustration, the feeling like you're going in circles, you tell yourself that the house was good enough for your parents and your grandparents, so why can't it be good enough for you? You remind yourself and your family that you're upholding a tradition.

Finally one day you realize that if you want to fix the house and keep it fixed, you'll need a more drastic approach: stripping the house of everything that's rotten and retrofitted to get down to its basic integrity, the solid foundation and sturdy beams upon which it was originally built; also you must tear up the yard to remove the invasive plants and debris, to allow its natural beauty to shine forth. You need to let go of tradition—the old forms, frames, and quirks that made the house familiar and also left it in perpetual disarray.

That describes the psychotherapeutic profession's general approach to mental health. Week after week, we go to our counselor to investigate the old storage shed out back, the old memories, and see if we can get some new awareness or technique installed in order to get the old house functioning a little better. Of course, slapping the new on the old is seldom a good fit, so we have to keep going back for adjustments or replacements.

There is another way.

So where do we start? The beginning is the end. We need to start by quitting—abandoning all that has not worked for us. Yes, I said *all*. This is a relationship issue, and everything is related to everything else. If I abuse alcohol, odds are I have alcoholic friends, along with a stressful work or living situation that drives me to use alcohol as an escape (I may also have inherited a family legacy of alcohol abuse), and I've probably created rituals around my alcohol consumption. It all has to go—cold turkey (see *#2*). It's the most assured way to break from our pattern.

How Therapists Can Help

Still, no matter the limitations of talk therapy, it is not going to vanish overnight. The model itself is bound to endure for some time even as individuals can make the choice to quit. There are some who realize talk therapy's limitations and still continue turning to it, as they know of no viable alternatives. This decision doesn't have to represent a dead end, though—and here is where enlightened therapists can help.

I am working on a trauma healing book with a woman who bemoans talk therapy. She recently told me about her dream to work herself out of her talk therapist job. Yet she doesn't have a magic pill to immediately accomplish that. Her approach is to not accept long-term clients, and instead to connect them as quickly as possible with non-verbal healing approaches that directly address their root imbalances.

I have witnessed five counseling sessions that have accomplished her goal in a single session or less. I hold them as models for what can be done here and now. While this approach is not a permanent fix, it allows us to make the best of what our culture currently offers us. The following are the distinguishing characteristics of those sessions that helped both client and counselor to get right down to work and do it successfully.

The counselors' contributions:

* They sidestepped the chitchat and went right for what they knew was there and needed to be addressed.

- They avoided current situations and proceeded with a whole-life perspective, showing how family of origin and early childhood experiences set the behavioral patterns that were tripping their client up in the present.
- They unraveled the patterns without dealing with any people involved, which obviated the need to address victimization, guilt, blame, or forgiveness.
- They kept clients on track by steering them toward relevant awarenesses and away from limiting beliefs and patterned responses.

The clients' contributions:

- They came ready to take a hard look at themselves and make the necessary changes.
- They demonstrated their trust in the process by questioning their beliefs, letting down defenses, and giving their all to the session.
- They embraced the nonverbal tools provided them.
- They left the session thinking they had done the work themselves—which, in fact, they did.*

These clients and counselors accomplished as much or more in one sitting than could typically be achieved in months—and even years—of weekly appointments strung together like so many hopeful prayer beads. Clients who came into the session feeling victimized left feeling empowered. Each carried out with them a deep sense of self-knowing.

Yet it must be remembered that awareness is only the first step in healing—they still had to do the work. With the deep sense of self-knowing and the newfound understanding of their family dynamic, they gained the confidence and wherewithal to go forward and change their lives.

---

* This is vital, as it greatly increases the odds that the client follows through and changes behavioral patterns.

Chapter in a Page

Talk therapy stems from the core assumption that healing is intermittent, verbal, and best managed by a counselor. However, this model actually inhibits our healing. Brief and routinized talk therapy sessions keep us functional, yet disempowered. Burdened by budget, insurance, and scheduling constraints, therapy is ultimately just an economic transaction. For our hunter-gatherer ancestors, though, healing permeated daily life and community. The Healer and the one to be healed would dwell together in a place of no boundaries, a place of complete trust with no eye on the clock.

Talking is also counterproductive, as our core wound is rooted in our limbic mind. Words can't get us there, nor can they express it. Our ancestors understood that deep and lasting change must be effected nonverbally, in the limbic system where our long-term memories and core motivations dwell. Verbal language involves translating thoughts and feelings into words and phrases. Inevitably, something is lost in the process. Repeatedly verbalizing our trauma, dysfunctional behavior, and distorted views also imprints them more deeply in our long-term memory.

Despite its flaws, talk therapy remains prevalent due to our focus on rationality and verbal techniques, the financial incentive for long-term solutions, and our lack of authenticity combined with our penchant for self-deception. Deception and self-deception are natural human traits, yet they become a problem when we take the illusions too seriously or use them to manipulate others. Talk therapy falls short here, as authenticity is hard to talk about—it is a state of being.

The most effective way to enhance personal healing would be to quit our maladaptive behavior patterns cold turkey. Another option is to seek enlightened therapists. These counselors see the individual seeking therapy as a full person, not simply a client or a diseased body. They act as mentors, guiding the person to find truth and resolution. This process harnesses nonverbal healing approaches that directly address our root imbalances.

10: We Keep Relying on Talk Therapy

1   Donald Robertson, *The Philosophy of Cognitive-Behavioural Therapy (CBT): Stoic Philosophy as Rational and Cognitive Psychotherapy* (London: Karnac, 2010), 16.

2   Joshua K. Swift and Roger P. Greenberg, "Premature Discontinuation in Adult Psychotherapy: A Meta-Analysis," *Journal of Consulting and Clinical Psychology* 80, no. 4 (2012): 547.

3   Marna Barrett, et al., "Early Withdrawal From Mental Health Treatment: Implications for Psychotherapy Practice," *Psychotherapy: Theory, Research, Practice, Training* 45, no. 2 (2008): 247.

4   Jamie Chamberlin, "Are Your Clients Leaving Too Soon?" *Monitor on Psychology* 46, no. 4 (2014): 60.

5   Richard Broome, *Aboriginal Australians* (Sydney: Allen & Unwin, 1982), 67.

6   Charles Berger, *Interpersonal Communication* (Berlin: De Gruyter Mouton, 2014), 65.

7   Laura K. Guerrero and Kory Floyd, *Nonverbal Communication in Close Relationships* (Routledge, 2006), 56.

8   Peter J. Marston and Michael L. Hecht, "The Nonverbal Communication of Romantic Love," *The Nonverbal Communication Reader: Classic and Contemporary Readings* (1999): 284-89.

9   Laura K. Guerrero and Kory Floyd, *Nonverbal Communication in Close Relationships*, 56.

10 Thomas Szasz. "The Healing Word: Its Past, Present, and Future," *Journal of Humanistic Psychology* 38, no. 2 (1998): 8-20.

11 Lambrini Kourkouta, "Ancient Greek Psychotherapy for Contemporary Nurses," *Journal of Psychosocial Nursing and Mental Health Services* 40, no. 8 (2002): 36-39.

12 Lee T. Pearcy, "Diagnosis As Narrative in Ancient Literature," *The American Journal of Philology* 113, no. 4 (1992): 595-616.

13 Ibid.

14 Arthur C. Bohart and Karen Tallman, "The Active Client: Therapy as Self-Help," *Journal of Humanistic Psychology* 36, no. 3 (1996): 7-30.

15 Robert S. Feldman, James A. Forrest and Benjamin R. Happ, "Self-Presentation and Verbal Deception: Do Self-Presenters Lie More?" *Basic and Applied Social Psychology* 24, no. 2 (2002): 163-70.

16 J.M. Tyler and R.S. Feldman, "Deflecting Threat to One's Image: Dissembling Personal Information As A Self-Presentation Strategy," *Basic and Applied Social Psychology* 27 (2005): 371-78.

17 J.S. Lockhard and D.L. Paulhus, *Self-Deception: An Adaptive Mechanism?* (Englewood Cliffs, NJ: Prentice-Hall, 1988), 25.

18 J.S. Lockard and C.A. Mateer, "Neural Bases of Self-Deception," in *Self-Deception: An Adaptive Mechanism?* (Englewood Cliffs, NJ: Prentice-Hall, 1988).

19 D.J. Bem, "Self-Perception Theory," in *Advances In Experimental Social Psychology*, no. 6 (1972): 1-62.

20 R.E. Nisbett and L. Ross, *Human Inference: Strategies and Shortcomings of Human Judgment* (Englewood Cliffs, NJ: Prentice-Hall, 1980), 201.

21 Ashley Merryman and Po Bronson, *NurtureShock: New Thinking About Children* (Twelve, 2011), 80.

22 Robert S. Feldman, James A. Forrest, and Benjamin R. Happ, "Self-Presentation and Verbal Deception: Do Self-Presenters Lie More?" *Basic and Applied Social Psychology* 24, no. 2 (2002): 163-70.

23 Jeffry Simpson, Jeffry and Douglas T. Kenrick, "Social Perception," *Evolutionary Social Psychology* (Mahwah, NJ: Lawrence Erlbaum Associates, 1997), 37.

24 William Von Hippel and Robert Trivers, "Chapter 4: Self-Deception to Deceive Others?" in *Social Thinking and Interpersonal Behavior*, eds. Joseph P. Forgas, Klaus Fiedler, and Constantine Sedikides (New York: Psychology, 2013), 65-80.

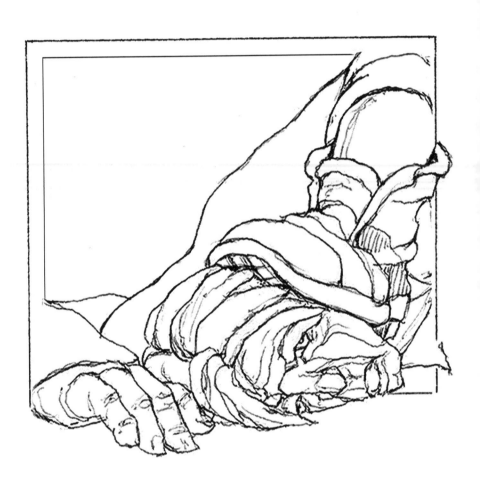

11: We Play the Pain Game

Those of you who know me as a storyteller and wilderness skills instructor might be wondering why I would know anything about pain, especially emotional pain. Pain of any kind is multifaceted. It affects a person's sense of self, interpersonal relationships, cultural identity, and even worldview—while each of these in turn influences the experience of the pain.[1] It unfolds as a character in a person's life story. To understand the pain, we need to know the stories that we tell about it; to resolve the pain, we need to know what it means to rewrite those stories.

The wilderness has provided me with a rich setting for this task. Anyone who has taught skills in a primitive living situation can tell you that they often end up doing more counseling than anything else. You can't get far with foraging, shelter building, and orienteering skills unless you can guide people through the discomfort thresholds, limiting beliefs, and dysfunctional relationship patterns that typically trip them up shortly after they step out of their comfort zones. In a primitive camp, you have to function independently and responsibly, without the crutches of accustomed routines and escapes. Your old stories inevitably begin to unravel, and you are faced with the opportunity to rewrite them.

Much of this book has involved getting out of our heads and into our hearts, though when it comes to dealing with pain, we need to do just the opposite, as the true source of our pain is mental.

Consider dental school, where students learn that it is the tooth and *also* the mind that creates pain. They learn a technique for tricking the mind, which goes like this: I tell my dentist that I have pain in my second lower molar on the left side. She investigates by saying, "I'm pressing on the first molar; do you feel any pain?" She then says, "Now I'm pressing on the second molar; do you feel any pain?" followed by, "I'm now pressing on the third molar." In actuality, she was pressing on teeth in a sequence other than what was stated, in order to see whether my teeth might say something different than my mind.

The story of our pain can be ambiguous and deceiving, yet there is also wisdom in it. Rather than denying the pain or despising ourselves for feeling it, we can tell the story of our pain as something more than a discrete physiological experience—as more than just a toothache—or something purely *bad*. The difference is dramatic and, as with most things, it comes down to a matter of perspective. Here's a story for inspiration:

Every day an Elder followed the path down to the stream to get water, which she brought back in two rawhide buckets on the ends of a pole she carried across her shoulders. One of the buckets had a tear in it, while the other was perfect. By the time the woman made it back to her lodge, the torn bucket would be half empty.

Four years passed, and each day the intact bucket grew more proud of himself for being able to deliver a full measure of water. "I am ashamed of myself," said the torn bucket. "I am a failure: This tear in my side lets water leak out all the way back up the trail."

The Elder looked over to him, laid her hand upon his damaged, water-stained skin, and said with a kindly smile, "Have you noticed all the Herbs and Flowers that now grow on the left side of the trail? And look at the Mice and Birds and Butterflies who have come to live there. The right side of the trail is still dry and dusty, since I have always carried you on the left—my gifting side—which is closest to my heart. Rather than seeing you as wounded and me carrying the pain of your imperfection when you arrived half empty day after day, I saw you as half full and overflowing with generosity. You trusted.

You shared your gift with many. In the way that giving is receiving, you made your pain your strength. I myself, as well as countless other beings, have been bathed in your blessings."

The solution to pain may be simple, while the process may not be. It could be miraculously quick. Most often, though, it takes time and tremendous dedication. The usual evolution to a new belief system occurs not as a steady progression—it happens in fits and starts. The stronger your vision and supportive community, and the more trust you have in them, the faster your transformation. Still, no matter the speed, the release from physical and emotional bondage is truly a miracle.

To Avoid the Pain Game

From an animal perspective, pain is pain. Our organism does not distinguish between emotional or physical. It is only our dichotomous, segregating mind that bothers with such trivial pursuits. You might already be aware that what you initially recognize as emotional pain has a physical component as well, and vice versa. Indeed, it is difficult to *not* reflect emotionally on our physical pain or to avoid feeling physically pained by a strong emotion.

Whether you recognize your pain as emotional or physical, it exists for the same reason. Pain is no more than a signal that something needs to be tended to. If you get your finger too close to a flame and feel pain, the reason for that pain is to convince you to withdraw your finger. If you did not feel pain, you would probably burn yourself. Maybe severely. The pain we feel is there to protect us from more pain. It is a gift without which we would probably not long survive.

I am not suggesting that we smile through moments of severe, or even minor, physical pain as if we weren't hurting at all—this pain exists, and it is distressing. We limit our perspective, though, when we think pain is *only* hurting, or worse, entirely without meaning. In other words, we make pain an issue when we treat it as an affliction unto itself. In doing so, we inadvertently do two things: We create more pain, and we distract our attention from the cause of the pain.

The same is true of what we commonly label *emotional pain*. This pain is uncomfortable, disturbing, heartbreaking, angering, and any number of other things. And we typically do everything we can to escape it. Just as with physical pain, we make the biggest mistake by not cherishing emotional pain when it comes—by not embracing it and asking it to sit in front of us and tell us its story. The more we welcome our emotional pain and listen to it, the less pain we are going to experience. Whenever you doubt that truth, think of what would happen if you were to stick your finger in that candle flame and deny the pain.

Reimagining Pain

Beauty exists in the story of pain. Pain isn't necessarily beautiful in the moment it arises, the feelings it generates, or even in the memory it leaves. Rather, it is beautiful in what it can mean and what it can teach us. It is no coincidence that both of these things depend solely on our perception. Part of the beauty of pain, you could say, is the way it becomes a reflection of who we are and how we want to be.

Here's another way of looking at it:

- To be unsatisfied is to be in a position to find satisfaction.
- To be cold is to be in a position to find warmth.
- To be in pain is to be in a position to heal.

If we deny that we are in pain, we are also denying ourselves the chance to heal. When I am seeking satisfaction, warmth, or healing, I am engaged in my own life process. I become sensitized to my feelings, my needs. I explore possibilities to see what works. In the process, I gain knowledge, learn skills, and grow in relationship.

When I live in that way (what I call the *Teaching Trail*), it feels good to lay my head down at night. It's not just the end of another day; it's the end of a day that I have lived to the fullest. I have taken what the day had to give, and I've given what the day asked of me. At the end of such a day, I notice that sleep comes easy, rest is deep, and I expect to wake up the next day brimming with passion, anxious to jump out of bed.

Responding to Physical Pain

Even after we have reimagined pain, we still have to confront it. The following two-step method can help us do so in a meaningful way.

1. **Acknowledge the pain.** If I am thirsty, yet I avoid it, I become dehydrated, and my thirst becomes chronic, unrelenting. The same happens with pain when we avoid it. When we listen to our pain right away by responding to it rather than trying to avoid or repress it, we take care of its cause. On the other hand, when we suppress the pain, our body has no choice other than to amp up the signal, i.e., to invoke more pain, in an effort to get us to take care of the cause.

2. **Move with the pain.** Rather than reading the pain as a call to limit movement, I'll now read it as a request to restore full movement. Unless it's an unhealed broken bone or a condition where movement actively jeopardizes your safety, you need to move when you have pain. It's not a move that is going to stress you; it's a move that's going to stretch and help the blood to get to that area, relax it, and nourish it.

Let's say that I have broken a bone, though—my arm, for instance. The pain I feel in this case is there to tell me "Take care of this arm, don't use it for things." If I'm not listening for that wisdom, then all I discern is extreme physical discomfort that leaves me feeling victimized by my own body and ultimately self-identifying with the pain. Remember, though: *Pain comes from the mind. It is based on input from the body, yet it doesn't come from the body.*

When the bone has healed, I may then encounter phantom pains that the synapses are trained to fire whenever I do something with this arm. In that situation, I can either live according to the pain, even though there is no physiological basis for it anymore, or I can work through it. Here's where I need to embrace the pain, which is actually embracing my fear of helplessness and long-term suffering, and power through it, work through it.

When I move my arm the way my brain warned against for so long by pushing the pain button, I start disconnecting the button's neural wiring. Even though there is pain, I gently explore the formerly forbidden movement area by allowing my body to intuitively find its own way around it. My body knows what to do: It has the genetic programming from a long evolutionary history of natural movement.

The Fast Track to Healing Emotional Pain

When pain receptors in the body are stimulated, we suffer, plain and simple. However, we are much more in control of our emotional reactions. It does not have to make us sad and depressed. It is a gift, like physical pain, intended to make us aware. Here are two tips for how to embrace emotional pain and take control of it:

1. **Remember that the mind's emotional responses are governed by a belief system**, which we can consciously change; I can either be happy or distraught over my son joining the military, depending on my political or religious convictions. Now imagine someone showing interest in your lover. Perhaps you feel insanely jealous—a common response for people in our culture. Yet if you were a member of a native culture patterned after the gifting way, you might feel honored and glad to share. Eliminating emotional pain can be as simple as changing my beliefs. I've watched vegetarians who got sick at the smell of

meat grow to savor it and seemingly heartless soldiers become caring pacifists, simply by changing their belief systems.

2. **Set an intention for yourself.** Think of yourself as having two bodies—a pain body and a joy body. When you wake up in the morning, you determine which one you move with that day. Dwelling in the joy body does not necessarily mean that we are always happy. We can be sad and experience flashes of anger or jealousy yet remain in our joy body. We are removed from the joy body when we experience our emotions through the lens of victimization. Staying in the joy body is a matter of remaining centered: empowering ourselves to listen to our feelings without judgment and make the changes to mollify those feelings.

WHEN OTHERS ARE IN PAIN

This is an intensely personal journey, which is why rescuing people from pain, though perhaps motivated out of compassion, is actually depriving them of the teaching that could keep them from future pain. At the same time, we need to be careful not to trigger fear of abandonment and feed the feeling of hopelessness that many chronic pain sufferers already harbor. Give them this chapter to read so that they understand how you are acting empathetically and wanting to work with them in turning around their relationship with pain.

Some Truth about Painkillers

Modern painkillers are touted as wonder drugs—they help us live with everyday banes ranging from migraines to lower back pain. Where would many of us be without them? Yet, the bigger question is where do many of us end up *with* them?

When we suppress pain, it allows us to go on with our normal affairs. What a godsend that would be—*if* suppression were normal. Pain suppression creates the illusion of wellness. The cause of the pain is still there, yet we go on functioning as though all is well.

Without the pain to moderate our actions, we often end up over-extending ourselves and hurting ourselves even worse. We then take more painkillers, risking physical degradation, drug dependence, or addiction.

The same is true with psycho-emotional painkillers, otherwise known as antidepressants. When we suppress the pain, we allow ourselves to continue the behaviors and relationships that originally caused the pain. In doing so, we sidestep the healing process that could mitigate the pain. This can result in increased dependence on medication, which as with painkillers, can lead to addiction.

All that, and for what? As we mentioned in #8, quite often the effect of chemical antidepressants is weaker than the placebo effect.[2] There is also evidence that antidepressants, compared to treatment with a placebo, *increase* a person's likelihood of suicide.[3]

Research has also shown that chronic lower back pain can be successfully treated with behavioral therapy—changing our cognitive processes and the ways we behave in relation to pain—with better results than traditional methods.[4]

Whether it be physical or mental pain, there is no easy fix. I suggest considering painkillers and antidepressants only for immediate relief, to give you the time and wherewithal for addressing the *cause* of the pain.

Explaining Chronic Pain

Acute pain is regarded as a universal phenomenon in human societies, even though the ways we experience, explain, and treat pain are exquisitely diverse.[5] However, chronic pain—when pain persists beyond the healing phase—is *not* universal, whether in terms of culture or time period.[6] It is also largely a conundrum for medical professionals, as the pain often does not seem to be explained biologically or physically.[7]

What we do know is that our emotions affect the experience of pain and can even worsen it.[8, 9, 10, 11] There is also evidence to suggest that emotions may play a role in causing chronic lower back pain.[12]

What we experience as chronic physical pain can be broken down into two distinct and complementary emotional responses:

1. Chronic anger
2. Chronic stress

Chronic anger is nothing more than anxiety on steroids. We feel anxious and we lose centeredness, which leaves us angry and feeling out of control, which leads to more anxiety, which leads to more anger. These emotional responses then begin to cause inflammation throughout the entire body. Chronic stress has a similar effect. It keeps hormonal levels elevated, which causes long-term muscle tension, joint stiffness, elevated pulse, and shortness of breath. Here's where chronic lower back pain and many other unexplainable joint and muscle pains come in.

We are designed to function in a state of dynamic relaxation, though when our anxiety, anger, or stress becomes chronic, we are functioning from a state of dynamic tension. The tension we feel tends to follow the path of least resistance, which takes it directly to the weakest or most compromised part of our system and produces pain.

It's as though we have turned on ourselves and begun tearing ourselves down. Think of it as running a machine nonstop at high speed. No machine is designed for that—sooner or later, it is going to overheat and start showing signs of fatigue. For the human machine, this could manifest as chronic fatigue syndrome and perhaps be a contributing factor to various forms of neuromuscular and cardiovascular disease, if not the primary cause.

Addressing Chronic Pain

Once I saw a physical therapist named Peter to get some help for my ever-present sore neck. He examined me and said my neck was fine, that my problem was all in my brain. As he explained why, I nodded in agreement nearly the whole time—he was describing essentially what I had come to realize about chronic emotional pain. We talked for an hour, comparing healing approaches, his to physical pain and mine to emotional pain, and we found very little difference.

Most chronic pain, Peter stated, is not the result of injury; rather, it's the outcome of a life where nearly everything we do is based on repetition. We train ourselves to experience an endless loop of pain the same way we train for a routine that makes today no more than a photocopy of yesterday or the day before. We become accustomed to managing the pain instead of seeking to eliminate it.

After my neck injury, I continually held my neck in a position that would minimize the pain, which trained my brain to push the pain button whenever I turned my neck out of that position. Now, long after my neck is healed, my brain still pushes the pain button whenever I turn my neck in a certain way, yet now with no neural input from my neck. I have created a self-perpetuating cycle—every time I want to move, I feel pain, and every time I feel pain, I don't want to move—that may never end. If I were living a primitive outdoor life, my movements would be continually varied, so neurons wouldn't wire together. When my neck injury healed, the pain would naturally have left.

The same thing happens with emotional pain: After a while, those people who keep making me angry or jealous don't have to do whatever it is that triggers me anymore; their mere appearance—or just the thought of them—causes those programmed neurons to automatically flick the pain switch. Each of us has around forty-five miles of nerves in our body, with a significant part of our circulatory system being devoted to maintaining them. No wonder we can so easily end up being controlled—even victimized—by them.

The longer we have a pain and the longer we obey that pain and respond to it, the harder it is to get over it. We're going here for the cure—we want to break the self-feeding loop creating the anxiety and stress that started this whole mess to begin with. The process is best approached gently, as pushing too hard could cause the brain to further entrench itself in our already established pain patterns. Here is the three-step process:

1. Awareness
2. Detachment
3. Reprogramming

The most effective technique I have come across for the first step, *awareness,* is to externalize every single anxiety that comes up, right *when* it comes up. It needs to be done immediately; if we do not consciously do something right away about the anxiety, our ego is going to step in and do it for us, and we already know what that leads to.

Now the second question is: How do I detach from the anxiety? Here is what my colleagues and I have found to be the best-proven techniques:

- Act it out.
- Dance it out.
- Write about it.
- Tell it to a friend, a tree, a bird.
- Shout it out to the cosmos.
- Sing about it.
- Pray for its release.

Now for the third step: *reprogramming.* The key to long-term pain cessation is changing our perception to affirm that *When I hurt, it doesn't mean I have been harmed.* Knowing that the pain is all in my head rather than in my muscles (or emotions), I no longer have to let it limit what I do with my body or feelings. I can resume control of my life rather than being victimized by my pain telling me how to move or feel.

The self that lives according to the dictates of pain is not our core self. It is not our centered self. We don't deny the pain or pretend it doesn't exist; we embrace it and remember that although it is real, pain is not who we are. We evade self-victimization, we quiet the defeatist self-talk, and we learn to move forward, choosing to set the pain aside with every step. Whether it is physical or emotional pain, it has fulfilled its mission, and it can now leave us.

Chapter in a Page

Much of this book urges us to get out of our heads and into our hearts, though with pain, we must do the opposite. The true source of pain is mental, so changing our experience of it means changing how we think about it.

Pain is pain. Our organism cannot distinguish between emotional or physical sensation. Only our dichotomous mind does that. You may notice that emotional pain has a physical component, and vice versa. Pain is just a signal that guides action to protect us from more pain.

We limit our perspective when we reduce pain to meaningless suffering. This only intensifies it and distracts us from the cause. Instead, remember the beauty: Pain isn't necessarily beautiful when it arises or even in memory; its beauty lies in what it teaches us. This depends on our perception of pain, which becomes a reflection of who we are and how we want to be.

To be in pain is to be in a position to heal. Deny our pain, and we also deny the chance to heal. When I acknowledge it, I am engaged in my own life process. I become sensitized to my feelings, my needs. I explore possibilities, gain knowledge, learn skills, and grow in relationship.

We can confront physical pain in two steps. First, acknowledge the pain. Second, move *with* the pain—not against it—to restore full movement. This movement rewires our neural connections and prevents phantom or chronic pain. Confront *emotional* pain by first remembering that a belief system triggers our emotional responses. Address these beliefs and listen to feelings without judgment or victimization.

A self that is molded by pain is not our core, centered self. Learn to embrace pain without identifying with it. Quiet defeatist self-talk and move forward while setting pain aside with every step. Whether physical or emotional, pain has fulfilled its mission when it leaves us with greater awareness of ourselves.

11: We Play the Pain Game Endnotes

1 Arthur Kleinman, *The Illness Narratives: Suffering, Healing, and the Human Condition* (Basic Books, 1988), 74.

2 Gary Greenberg, "Manufacturing Depression," *Harpers Magazine*, last modified May 2007, accessed 20 October 2020, http://harpers.org/archive/2007/05/manufacturing-depression/.

3 S. Nassir Ghaemi, P.A. Vohriner and E.A. Whitham, "Antidepressants from a Public Health Perspective: Re-Examining Effectiveness, Suicide, and Carcinogenicity," *Acta Psychiatrica Scandinavica* 127, no. 2 (2013): 89-93.

4 Nicholas Henschke, et al., "Behavioural Treatment for Chronic Low-Back Pain," *Cochrane Database Syst. Rev.* 7, no. 7 (2010).

5 Paul E. Brodwin, "Introduction," in Mary-Jo DelVecchio, *Pain as Human Experience: An Anthropological Perspective* (Berkeley: U of California, 1992), 1-28.

6 Ibid.

7 Ibid.

8 H. Schubiner, "Emotional Awareness for Pain," *Integrative Medicine* (2018): 963-70.

9 N. Henschke, et al., "Behavioural Treatment for Chronic Low-Back Pain," *Cochrane Database Syst Rev.*, no. 7 (2010): CD002014.

10 R.J. Smeets, et al., "Chronic Low Back Pain: Physical Training, Graded Activity with Problem Solving Training, or Both? The One-Year Post-Treatment Results of a Randomized Controlled Trial," *Pain* 134, no. 3 (2008): 263-76.

11 K. Kroenke, et al., "Optimized Antidepressant Therapy and Pain Self-Management in Primary Care Patients with Depression and Musculoskeletal Pain: A Randomized Controlled Trial," *JAMA 301, no. 20 (2009): 2099-2110.*

12 Marwan N. Baliki, et al., "Chronic Pain and the Emotional Brain: Specific Brain Activity Associated with Spontaneous Fluctuations of Intensity of Chronic Back Pain," *The Journal of Neuroscience* 26, no. 47 (2006): 12165-73.

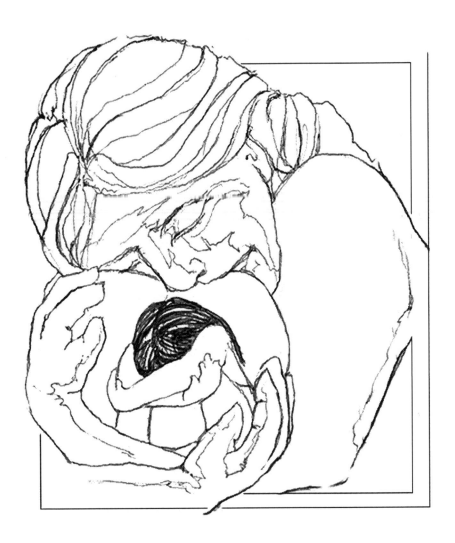

12: We Forgive

In #9 we mentioned Wilfred Pelletier's claim that our culture is built on an enemy concept, in which our relationships and policies are consistently framed as a fight against an enemy.[1] On the one hand, this leads us to create enemies where they do not exist. On the other, it introduces a power dynamic into our relationships in the form of forgiveness, which we either bestow upon our "enemies" or withhold from them.

It is commonly believed that forgiveness is healing in and of itself. However, in my experience, forgiveness-derived healing is a short-term illusion. I got stroked by the person's acceptance of my forgiveness. Yet what have I really gained? Merely an ego boost from feeling *right* and exerting power over someone. The high feeling soon wears off, and the forgiven person either harbors resentment for feeling unacknowledged and misunderstood, or he assumes a second-class role as a moral inferior. As we'll discuss shortly, forgiveness can impede healing and distract us from where our attention should be: acceptance and empathy.

Reinforcing Victimization

We know from the previous chapter that storytelling is critical to understanding human pain. It is also key to addressing what is wrong with forgiveness. By age two, humans are already narrating and evaluating past experiences.[2] Throughout the course of our lives, we are both characters and storytellers, actively influencing the framing of these experiences.

In order to forgive, there must be both a victim and a perpetrator. When we label someone else a perpetrator, we reflexively cast ourselves as the victim in our story. This pigeonholing results in two outcomes:

1. **It creates a distance between the perpetrator and the victim**, which limits the healing and the manifestation of empathy that may still be possible. This distance is vertical rather than horizontal: The victim assumes the moral high ground, and the perpetrator is relegated to the moral cesspool. In simple terms, the victim is right, and the perpetrator is wrong. From this righteous position, the victim bestows forgiveness.

2. **We get caught up in the roles of perpetrator and victim**, which leads us to forget about the humanity in both. We are then less likely to act from a place of empathy.

Studies of victim and perpetrator narratives of the same event find that the victim's perspective endures longer than the perpetrator's.[3] The experience of victimhood becomes entrenched, and forgiveness reinforces that narrative, as the prerequisite for offering forgiveness is seeing ourselves as having been victimized.

Blame, shame, and forgiveness together perpetuate the victimization cycle. Whether I am laying blame on someone, shaming her into taking blame, or forgiving her for the blame she has already assumed, it's all the same—I am taking the moral high ground. Where the perpetrator had the upper hand over me, I now rise over her. With morality/God/truth/justice on my side, I have reversed the hierarchy: I have cast the perpetrator in the role of victim, though at the same time, I have made myself another kind of perpetrator.

Moving Beyond the Victim Narrative

I became enlightened fifteen years ago when working with Hurricane Carter, Lois Einhorn (recipient of the World Forgiveness Alliance's

Heroine of Forgiveness, Reconciliation, and Peace award), Arun Gandhi (Mahatma Gandhi's grandson), Derrick Jensen, Daniel Quinn, Pete Seeger, Bernie Siegel, Kurt Waldheim (past UN Secretary-General), and forty others on a forgiveness and child abuse research project.[4] From that experience, I refrain from using the words *victim* and *perpetrator* due to the connotations they carry. When we can start using those words in reference to the *pattern* rather than the person, we can begin the deep healing that goes beyond mere management and beyond unconsciously perpetuating the pattern.

Let's be clear here: There are definitely victims in this world—millions of them. And there are clear and obvious perpetrators. The problem with our healing arises when we:

1. **Assume** either the victim or perpetrator role

2. **Treat** that role as our whole identity

3. **Focus** on ourselves or the other instead of the relationship between us

If I am sexually violated as a child by an adult, I am clearly the victim in the relationship. However, once I am an adult, I can begin to take personal responsibility for my actions by desisting from playing the victim role. In this way, I empower myself and keep from getting hurt.

The line between victim and perpetrator could then start to fade, as I am now able to see that my childhood perpetrator was a victim herself when she was a child. What she did to me was what her perpetrator taught her to do. I might also start seeing how I played out my own victim conditioning by lashing out and victimizing others. Also, I can reflect on times when I took the moral high ground by sympathizing with the victim and blaming the perpetrator.

Playing the victim-perpetrator game stymies my personal development and puts my healing at a standstill. I am locked in a dichotomous perspective: Either I am right or wrong, free or enslaved, morally upright or deplorable. I remain locked in my ego, either defending myself or aggressing against another's defendedness. In a dichotomous world, it is impossible to just be—I have to be right, otherwise I am wrong. It is impossible to be as a question when I have to have an answer—the *right* answer.

When I am able to step beyond the victim-perpetrator dichotomy, I can observe how dynamic these roles are and how they often intersect. In our culture, we tend to believe that the victim is always and entirely the victim, while the perpetrator is always and entirely the perpetrator. The reality, though, is more nuanced.

If you need more reflection on this subject, I suggest that you consult a therapist who specializes in victimization and forgiveness work.

The Language of Forgiveness

The American Heritage Dictionary defines the verb *forgive* as the decision "to give up resentment against or stop wanting to punish someone for an offense or fault; pardon."[5] The catch here is that an offense or fault is committed only if someone is judged as having done so. There is no objective standard we can appeal to—it's all subjective. The mere fact that I have taken a bushel of apples from my neighbor's tree does not mean that I have committed an offense. This is up to my neighbor to determine. Knowing my need, she might condone the act and perhaps offer me more apples. Another neighbor might judge me as guilty of stealing.

Even though the second neighbor may forgive me, he still first judged me as guilty. If he had not, there would have been no reason to forgive. *There is no forgiveness, therefore, without judgment.*

We can't talk about forgiveness without also talking about apology. *The American Heritage Dictionary* defines the verb *apologize* as "to make excuse for or regretful acknowledgment of a fault or offense."[6] It is forgiveness and judgmentalism coming from the opposite direction—this time rising from the moral cesspool. The perpetrator judges himself as wrong and the victim as right, then acknowledges this to the victim.

Several years ago, a friend wrote me a letter of apology when she thought she had offended me. I replied, "An apology is not something you have to express to me. I feel that most people are doing the best they can at any particular time, so to be sorry for what you've done is to be sorry for doing your best."

The act of apologizing does not take into account that how someone *reacts* has more to do with what she perceived was done to her than what actually occurred. Nor does it acknowledge the control we have over our lives, our beliefs, and our perceptions. Judgment, whether of ourselves or others, is the last thing we need if we are genuinely seeking personal healing. The reason is that *forgiveness and apology, which are seemingly innocuous and supposedly virtuous acts, are both candy-coated judgments.*

Several commonly practiced examples are listed in the following chart, along with explanations of their hidden attachments, followed by suggestions for healthy alternatives.

Virtuous Action	Hidden Attachment Motivation	Non-attachment Alternative
Sympathy	Superiority. When I sympathize, I assume that I am more privileged.	Empathy
Forgiveness	Judgment. When I forgive, I come from a place of moral superiority.	Acceptance
Gift-giving	Control. When I care how a gift is used or who ends up with it, I manipulate.	Gifting with no strings attached
Gratitude	Judgment. When I express appreciation, I am evaluating a gift instead of receiving it.	Receiving with no appraisal
Advice	Conversion. When I try to influence, I want someone to think or do as me.	Listening, mirroring

Is Forgiveness Natural?

Terms for *apology* and *forgiveness* are rarely found in the languages of indigenous peoples. Seminole Medicine Man Sonny Billie says, "In our language there is no word to say, 'I'm sorry' … The white man has lots of words for 'I'm sorry.'"[7] Such terms are unusual in Native languages since people who are directly engaged with the means and ends of their existence have neither the room nor the incentive to play the victimization game. If someone were to assume the moral high ground necessary to bestow forgiveness, she would risk being ostracized. The same would be true of someone who humiliated himself and risked the welfare of his people by continually playing victim.

When Moravian missionaries were working among the Inuit of Eastern Canada, they ran into an issue early on: The Natives had no word for forgiveness. This posed a serious limitation to the missionaries, as forgiveness is a—if not *the*—core concept of Christianity. The missionaries had to construct a seven-syllable word, *issumariyungnaerpok*,[8] to get something close to the concept of forgiveness across to them. Still, the English equivalent of the behemoth is closer to *forget* than *forgive*.

THE CHI DEBWEWEN TEST

The Elders suggested to me these tools for identifying Chi Debwewen:
1. Observation, revelation, and direct experience
2. Verification within my realm of existence and those of other humans, cultures, and times
3. Verification within the dominion of nature

In the Ojibwe tradition in which I was trained, there is *Debwewen*, which is personal truth, and *Chi Debwewen*, which is the universal truth. A person who wants to know if his or her knowledge or beliefs are Chi Debwewen tests them by applying them to a variety of people and situations. I did this with *forgiveness* in order to gain some insight into whether or not it is a natural human trait. Reasoning that hunter-gatherer peoples would represent the essential human, I applied Chi Debwewen to a number of native groups from around the world.

I had no trouble finding apparent Native references to forgiveness. The Awabakal Aborigines of southeast Australia have a term, *Wa-re-kul-li-ko*, which means *to forgive*. The term *Antaa* is reported to mean the same in the language of the Saami (Laplanders) of northern Scandinavia. These findings seemed to contradict what I learned from my friendships with people of these cultures, whom I would not describe as particularly forgiving. This drew me to these conclusions:

1. Language-based communication is imperfect and becomes more so when translated cross-culturally.

2. Observations are subject to interpretation, and all interpretations are subjective.

Consider the Ojibwe word *booni*, which some linguists translate as *forgive*, that merely means to *leave alone or not think about*. At the same time, *Ho'oponopono* is commonly known as the old Hawaiian practice of forgiveness, although the literal translation is *make good-good*, or simply *correct*. These precise translations speak of taking responsibility for one's actions—a matter of honor, whereas forgiveness is pardoning—a matter of perspective.

My community performs a Smudging Ceremony (an invocation and cleansing with herbal incense) before foraging or building a lodge. Some see this as asking forgiveness for disturbing the land or killing plants, whereas the Elders explain it as asking if it is okay to be there, giving thanks for the privilege, and expressing intent to live in harmony and disturb as little as possible. The term *forgiveness*, then, is loosely applied to traditional cultural practices that have little to do with forgiveness as it is understood in the Judeo-Christian culture.

Why Forgiveness Emerged

Contemporary and historical hunter-gatherers (which includes our early ancestors) live and lived the Beauty Way. The Earth Mother provides virtually all necessities and desires, so there is no need for sustained labor, forming governments, or accumulating wealth and possessions. With so little to cause regret, tension, or strife, there is little need for forgiveness.

When we humans became agriculturists, we had to deal with feast and famine, wealth and poverty, bureaucracy and plague, and work, work, work. Our lives rotated around routines of protracted toil in the fields. With little contentment in the present and much to cause the aforementioned regret, tension, and strife, we began to look to the future for respite and reward. We founded religions to support us and promise that our long suffering would be rewarded after death.

The concept of forgiveness is part and parcel of the world's major religious traditions. I found it at nearly every turn when exploring the Judeo-Christian tradition. Here is an instance from the Hebrew *Standard Prayer Book*: "Thou givest a hand to offenders, and thy right hand is stretched out to receive the penitent."[9] And here is one in Christianity's most popular prayer (from The Book of Common Prayer): "Forgive us our trespasses, as we forgive those who trespass against us."[10] The Hindu prayer to Bhu Devi is offered as an entreaty for forgiveness for stepping upon the Earth,[11] and the contemporary Buddhist monk Beopjeong says that "The Buddha resides in a place of forgiveness."[12] The *Qur'an* of Islam states that "Allah is All-Pardoning, Ever-Forgiving," (Surat-Al-Hajj, 60) and "If someone pardons and puts things right, his reward is with Allah," (Surat-Ash-Shura, 40).[13] Even *A Book of Pagan Prayer* states that "If I have done anything to offend you [Ancestors] … I ask for forgiveness."[14]

In the context of religion, forgiveness often takes a transactional form: we offer forgiveness to others in order to receive divine forgiveness for ourselves. It is an exchange that is as much about self-interest as it is about mercy or empathy. We would be wise to remember that these exchanges, and the relationships built on them, are not of the same vein. Religious approaches to forgiveness serve as coping mechanisms for the misery of daily life in industrialist/agriculturalist cultures, right alongside sin, karma, meditation, tolerance, and justice. When people I know have returned to the Beauty Way, they have gradually abandoned these crutches, as they are no longer needed.

Quitting Forgiveness for Acceptance

Our culture puts a positive spin on forgiveness, which usually takes the form of the mantra *Forgive and forget*, or as Robert Browning said, "Good to forgive, best to forget."[15] Yet our woundedness is oftentimes so severe that these words fail to resonate. Our lives have been irrevocably altered, and the pain endures long after the incident that caused it. Forgive and forget is not good enough—we need answers.

I do not claim to have all the answers. However, I have learned the first step: acceptance. *With acceptance, we acknowledge the event and all parties involved, without the judgment.* We provide the groundwork for dialogue and understanding.

Forgiveness creates distance between the "victim" and "perpetrator," which makes us more likely to demonize one and deify the other. With acceptance, the line between victim and perpetrator fades, which encourages new perspectives. Some discover that the perpetrator has been (or still is) an abuse victim, or that the victim has become a perpetrator. I have witnessed miracles that I would previously never have imagined, such as both "victim" and "perpetrator" expressing thankfulness for an abuse incident since it proved pivotal in their awakening and subsequent healing.

With the acceptance approach, we honor the relationship of the people involved. Regarding childhood sexual abuse, the overwhelming majority of incidents occur within the context of established relationships. Focusing on the abuse itself is simply treating the symptom of an out-of-balance relationship, and it is seldom the only symptom. The core of the imbalance lies in the relationship, so the healing focus ought to be on the relationship rather than on a particular individual.

Barriers to Acceptance

Healing is energy, and the healing process requires the uninhibited flow of energy. Blockages often manifest as the result of these three conditions:

1. **We feel threatened or overwhelmed.** Very few of us, whether victim or perpetrator, abused or abuser, come by acceptance easily—especially when first introduced to the option. Shame and anger cloud our perspectives, and fears of vulnerability and accountability loom. This can make us suspicious of any outside involvement, so rather than seeing acceptance as a doorway to healing, we fear it is being dangled before us as bait to lure us into the usual blame-shame scenario. For these reasons, we need to spell out clearly exactly what we have to let go of, along with the benefits.

2. **We are attached to outcome and resistant to change**. When this is the case, we need to remember what it is that we *gain* from acceptance. With acceptance, we can acknowledge and allow the existence of something hurtful, even insidious, without needing to embrace or condemn it. This allows us to be involved in the relationships around the issue, and to learn from the experience in a personally safe and mutually supportive way. I also find it helpful to remind resistant individuals that the event is history, and that they are not being asked to go back and change anything. Acceptance is merely an acknowledgment of the relationships and individual truths involved. The more we resist, the more we involve ourselves. The very act of resisting is creating a bond—a relationship—with what we are trying to avoid.

3. **We want control.** Acceptance can be frightening since it is open-ended: There are no clues as to what course it might take, and there are no defined goals either. This is the beauty of acceptance: It requires us to be vulnerable, the first prerequisite for any healing to occur.

Acceptance is not a virtue, nor is it a religious ideal. It is a simple matter of practicality. Without acceptance, we are right back to judgmentalism in its various guises. Acceptance is healing in and of itself, both for the individual and the relationships involved. It does not mean agreement. It is merely a recognition and honoring of another person's reality, even though it may differ from our own. This includes past realities of our own that may not resonate with our present reality. In that case, acceptance of the incident can provide a giant step toward self-acceptance.

The Give-and-Take of Acceptance

In order to create space for our healing, we must release some clutter. As my Elders used to tell me, *Giving is receiving.* I saw it as a simple matter of physics: A full container cannot accept anything more. Yet they saw it as a matter of respect: You first honor someone by giving an offering, then you may be gifted in return. Here is how it relates to acceptance:

What We Give Up

- Expectations of forgiveness or being forgiven
- Desires for retribution or restitution
- Anonymity—both stories are known to others
- Being right—there are no sides
- Remaining a victim/perpetrator

What We Gain

- Acknowledging the relationship of all people involved
- Identifying the behavioral patterns that trigger the abuse
- Recognizing the generational history of the abuse
- Contributing to the self-esteem of both perpetrator and victim
- Encouraging trust
- Inviting others to help and support
- Opening to emotional honesty and the potential for true caring

The Role of Empathy

We have a saying in our culture: *To err is human, and to forgive is divine.* I would like to change that to *Forgiveness is judgment; empathy is divine.* And let us remember that—contrary to popular belief—*forgiveness* and *empathy* are not one and the same. Mark Twain is often quoted as saying that "Forgiveness is the fragrance a violet sheds on the heel that has crushed it."[16] Forgiveness is merely a kinder, gentler form of blame and judgment. It has become the tool by which our culture empowers victims and oppresses perpetrators. The price, however, is a two-dimensional view of human beings, where one person is entirely right and the other is entirely wrong, period. Forgiveness is about power, not about healing.

Empathy, on the other hand, just *is*—there is no overlay of expectation or perception. This allows us to see ourselves and others holistically and as part of a web of relationship, which is where both the problem and the healing are found.

Empathy does not deny the pain. Instead, it helps us to acknowledge it and, at the same time, transcend it.

Chapter in a Page

Forgiveness impedes healing and distracts from our ideal focus: acceptance and empathy. To forgive requires a victim and a perpetrator. When we label someone a perpetrator, we cast ourselves as victim. This pigeonholing causes two outcomes. First, the victim becomes morally superior to the perpetrator, which limits the potential for caring within the relationship. Second, we latch onto our victim-perpetrator roles and forget the humanity in both. This impairs empathy, and victims risk perpetuating the abuse cycle as perpetrators.

Still, there are definitely victims and perpetrators in this world. The problem arises when we cling to our assumed role as an identity and magnify the individuals instead of the relationship we share. When I step beyond the victim-perpetrator dichotomy, I can observe the nuance and dynamism of these labels—victims are seldom always and entirely the victim, and the perpetrator role isn't stable and immutable either.

Forgiveness depends on perceived offenses or faults. Therefore, forgiveness requires judgment, which is the least helpful thing for personal healing. In sum: *Forgiveness and the apologies that elicit it are both judgments masquerading as virtuous actions.* They are more about power than about connection, relationship, and mutual healing.

To heal, we must relinquish forgiveness and cultivate acceptance. This allows the existence of something hurtful without us needing to embrace or condemn it. We are engaged in the relationships around the issue, and we learn from experience in a safe and mutually supportive way. This new perspective encourages healing.

Acceptance doesn't mean agreement; it's merely a recognition and honoring of another person's reality. This includes reconciling our past with our present, which helps move us toward self-acceptance. Such an open-ended, uncharted, and goal-free process can be frightening. Yet this is the beauty of acceptance: It requires us to be vulnerable, which is the only way we can be open to healing.

12: We Forgive Endnotes

1 Wilfred Pelletier, "Childhood in an Indian Village" (Somerville, MA: New England Free Press).

2 Peggy J Miller and Linda L. Sperry, "Early Talk About the Past: The Origins of Conversational Stories of Personal Experience," *Journal of Child Language* 15, no. 2 (1988): 293-315.

3 Roy F. Baumeister, Arlene Stillwell, and Sara R. Wotman, "Victim and Perpetrator Accounts of Interpersonal Conflict: Autobiographical Narratives About Anger," *Journal of Personality and Social Psychology* 59, no. 5 (1990): 994.

4 Lois Einhorn, *Forgiveness and Child Abuse: Would You Forgive?* (Bandon, OR: Robert D. Reed Publishers, 2006).

5 "Forgive," *American Heritage Dictionary*, accessed 22 October 2020, https://www.ahdictionary.com/word/search.html?q=forgive&submit.x=58&submit.y=27.

6 "Apologize," *American Heritage Dictionary*, accessed 22 October 2020, https://www.ahdictionary.com/word/search.html?q=apologize&submit.x=25&submit.y=3.

7 Shirley Jones, *Simply Living: The Spirit of the Indigenous People*, 150.

8 Arthur Thibert, *Eskimo (Inuktitut) Dictionary* (New York, 2004), 177.

9 Simeon Singer," *The Standard Prayer Book: Conclusion Service for the Day of Atonement* (New York: Bloch Publishing Company, 1915), 411.

10 *The Book of Common Prayer* (New York: The Church Pension Fund, 1928), 3.

11 "Prayer to Bhu Devi," *Hindupedia, The Hindu Encyclopedia*, trans. P. R. Ramachander, accessed 18 Aug. 2015, http://www.hindupedia.com/en/Prayer_to_Bhu_Devi.

12 "Monk Stresses Forgiveness at Biannual Dharma Talk," *The Chosun Ilbo (English Edition): Daily News from Korea*. last modified 18 Apr. 2004,

accessed 22 October 2020, http://english.chosun.com/site/data/html_dir/2004/04/18/2004041861016.html.

13 "Verses of the Quran about Forgiveness - Harunyahya.com," *Harun Yahya*, accessed 22 October 2020, http://www.harunyahya.com/en/Articles/17230/verses-of-the-quran-about.

14 Ceisiwr Serith, *A Book of Pagan Prayer* (Weiser Books, 2002), 135.

15 Robert Browning, Charlotte Endymion Porter and Helen Archibald Clarke, *The Poems of Robert Browning* (Crowell, 1896), 434.

16 Ian Williamson and Marti Hope Gonzales (2007). "The Subjective Experience of Forgiveness: Positive Construals of the Forgiveness Experience," *Journal of Social and Clinical Psychology* 26, no. 4 (2007), 407-46.

Epilogue: What if …

At this point, you are likely asking yourself, "What would it be like to put it all together—to live without fear controlling me, without being trapped in old beliefs, without playing the pain game, without falling down the rabbit hole of depression? What would happen if I started to give what I wanted to receive, feed what I wanted to grow, and surround myself with what I wanted to become?"

Whether or not you think you are capable of doing so, you're right. You already know in your Heart-of-Hearts that joy and fulfillment come from keeping good company, nurturing your true self, and sharing with others what means most to you. Following is the story of a people who had the courage to abandon their old script. In doing so, they learned how liberating it was to live without what they once thought was indispensable, to bear what they once thought was intolerable, and to do what they once thought was impossible.

A tourist stopped at a quaint hotel in a charming peasant village. She laid a $100 bill on the front desk and asked the proprietor if she might take a look at the rooms to be sure there was one that suited her.

Unbeknownst to her, the village was struggling. Drought had descended upon the valley, and the village was so far off the beaten path that the rest of the region seemed to have forgotten about them. The hotel had fallen on hard times as well, as the road through the village was seldom traveled, and so few people in the outside world knew about this gem of a community from a bygone era tucked away in the mountains.

The hotel had fallen behind in payments to its suppliers. While the tourist was perusing the upstairs rooms, the proprietor—feeling confident that she would choose one of the nicely appointed rooms with an alluring view of the surrounding alpine peaks—quickly ran the $100 a couple of doors down to pay his friend the butcher, who supplied the hotel kitchen with fresh meat.

In turn, the butcher immediately went to pay her friend the herdsman, who supplied her with cows, chickens, and hogs. The herdsman lost no time taking the cash to pay his kindly neighbor, the bachelor farmer, who grew the hay and grain for his livestock. The farmer then right away went to settle his debt with the lady of pleasure who brought him comfort in the night. She, using the hotel to ply her trade, went directly there to settle for past visits.

Just as the lady left, the tourist came down the steps and told the clerk that as enchanting as the hotel was, she thought the better of halting her travels so early in the day. She picked up her $100 bill from where she left it and continued on her sightseeing amble up the valley.

Little did she know that she spread joy and a sense of hope throughout the village with her simple, trusting act of giving before receiving. And everyone benefited, without detriment to any one individual, as they each fed what they wanted to grow. Such is the Circle Way, where like begets like and we become what we surround ourselves with. The only cost was what would have closed their hearts, which meant letting go of boundaries fueled by fear, pain, and judgment.

At the same time, the rewards for the villagers extended far beyond the immediate and obvious. They strengthened relationship by seeing again how caring first for each other was at the same time caring for themselves. They each knew that they—as individuals and as a community—would benefit more from sharing than hoarding. The money was merely a symbol for what they truly shared: the nurturing and sense of security that comes from being immersed in the giving-receiving continuum.

From both hard experience and stories passed down by their Elders, the villagers were aware of the fact that the Circle Way worked in reverse as well. They knew that if just one person decided to put self-interest first and keep the money, the ripple effect would cause the entire community to suffer. Again, hoarding the money would have just been a symbol for exclusion, secrecy, gossip, judging, bullying, withholding affection, or anything else that supposedly hurt just one person.

The Hardest Question

I saved one particular "What if ..." for the very last, as I wouldn't know how to address it before you finished this book or if you had not come from a community such as the one in the story above. I face the same dilemma when a workshop participant or client poses the question when I first present the three steps to emotional freedom. The question usually goes something like this: "That all sounds well and good, but what if someone can't first give, because they simply have nothing *to* give? Or what if they're not capable of feeding what they want to grow? And what about someone who doesn't have access to the caliber of people they want to emulate?"

The hypothetical "someone" usually turns out to be the questioner. The reason for the nebulous third person and for the question starting with a distancing "What if" is that in most cases, the questioner has cultivated a persona of normalcy to mask his deeply wounded self, and he does not want to risk exposure.

"Oh, that's not me!" some of you are going to say. I've said it myself. Our defensiveness points to the likelihood that—consciously or not—we are lying to ourselves. Odds are that we are maintaining rigid self-protective boundaries and that we lean on either belief systems or addictive behaviors (or both) to keep us afloat. So armored, we go through our days in fight-flight mode. Closeness with others is never deeply satisfying.

Our survival becomes dependent on a me-first approach to life. To give before receiving or to surround ourselves with people more conscious than ourselves would be opening a frightful crack in the armor we so carefully installed around us.

Let's now return to our "That's not me" statement. Many of us are not consciously aware of the fact that we are one of "them." We don't see our loneliness as the fallout of our survival strategy. We have masked our self-focus in the poetry of pleasant-sounding terms like personal empowerment, self-realization, abundance consciousness, self-fulfillment, assertiveness training, self-help, and improving self-worth.

My last words to you are an imploration to take a leap of faith and trust in the open, caring person you really are. Lay that $100 bill on the counter and walk away from it. Whether it's there when you get back or not, know that you have created an opening for something infinitely more valuable.

Oh, there's one more "What if ..." What if it doesn't work? You can always go back to your old life, but I doubt you will even entertain the thought after what you discover.

The Book in a Couple of Pages

Healing begins—and ends—with the same realization: We are already healed. We may have dysfunctional behavioral or relationship patterns, yet we ourselves are not intrinsically dysfunctional. It is on the journey from beginning to end that we awaken to our core self, our healed self, and adapt our beliefs, behaviors, and relationships to it. The Path is not linear and there is no finish; it is a continual process of growth and rebirth. There are many beginnings and many ends.

Your personal healing journey is not about your parents, your upbringing, or your inner child—it is about *you*, in this moment. Although the journey is unique to each of us, we all share two things:

1. **The beginner's mind:** an open, nonjudgmental perspective in which we are ready to be challenged, learn, and receive. We are willing to reexamine our preconceived beliefs, cultural idols, and core wound.

2. **Acceptance:** We honor our past and our pain, whether physical or emotional. We remember that to be in pain is to be in a position to heal. If we deny our pain, we are also denying ourselves the chance to heal and engage in our life process.

We like to think that we are rational beings, guided by intellect. The truth is that we are first emotional beings, with intellectual capacities second. Living a life that is whole and healed means living from the heart, which does not mean we are living irrationally, only that we are using the rational mind to serve the heart.

As we do so, we also begin to embrace the subjectivity of life. We give ourselves permission to cherish and honor our personal truths as well as the truths of others, even if they are different from our own.

We recognize that there is no objectivity—that every thought and feeling I have, every desire and impulse, is biased, and is biased since it is my own, which is the only thing it should be.

Health and wellness are personal. They are also an everyday affair, which means we need to take personal responsibility for our well-being *and* that of those close to us. In the Circle Way, we are responsible to each other. Life is not about us as individuals; it is about our relationships. True healing takes place in this web of relationships—not in a therapist's office—and our true healing partners are those with whom we share daily life, those who help us break patterned behaviors or further entrench them.

The healing itself is premised on three things:

1. **We give what we want to receive.** We are all connected in the Web of Life. When I support you in your healing, I support myself in my own healing.

2. **We feed what we want to grow.** We give attention and energy to what we desire rather than focusing on what we do not desire.

3. **We surround ourselves with what we want to become.** When we stay put in our surroundings, we stay stuck; when our surroundings change, we change.

In the moments when we are feeling most lost, when self-doubt looms overhead and every step feels uncertain, we turn to honor and respect. To honor is to create space for listening, and respect is the actual listening. No matter where I am, who I am with, or what little I have, I am always in a position to give these two things. And when I give, I can receive, and I find my way again on the Path to healing.

Glossary

acceptance: A recognition and honoring of someone else's or our own **Truth**.

Adam and Eve Syndrome: Inner conflict due to the **limbic mind** and **rational mind** being out of sync, exacerbated by our hyper-rational culture.

archetype: A pattern of energy emanating from the **limbic mind**, often manifesting as a role or personality type.

authenticity: An expression of the **true self** emanating from the **limbic mind.**

Balance: The state of personal centeredness that results from following inner guidance and living in harmony with life.

Beauty Way: A way of life that allows one to remain centered and not only see, but also benefit from all in life that appears beyond control.

be as a question: To live with an openness to all possibilities; to avoid assumptions.

beginner's mind: To drop all preconceived notions about a subject or activity before studying or participating.

boundaries: The physical, emotional and mental limits we establish to protect ourselves from harm; they are more necessary in our culture of scarcity than while living in the **Hoop of Life**.

Chi Debwewen: Universal truth.

Circle: A community that works interdependently rather than hierarchically, recognizing the value and equal importance of every person's role in the group.

Circle Consciousness: Heart-generated thinking and feeling that takes into account the **Hoop of Life**; allows transcendence of the ego to accommodate the needs of others along with personal needs.

Circle Way: The manner in which all things are related to, and affect, each other.

codependency: Reliance on another person for approval and identity, which in turn supports that person's dysfunctions.

core emotions: The four emotions that underlie every other emotion—**fear, longing, sadness,** and **joy.**

core wound: A deep-seated, universal sense of shame that develops early in childhood, resulting in denial of our **true self** and development of an ego-based self image.

Debwewen: Personal **Truth.**

depression: A culturally classified mental illness; a passive expression of chronic **fear** and **sadness,** characterized by lack of sleep, poor concentration, self-criticism, guilt, and suicidal thoughts.

Dreamself: The aspect of self that communicates to us through our dreams.

Dreamtime (collective unconscious, spirit world, astral plane)

ego: The aspect of personality that creates self-consciousness and individual identity; our **fear**-based identity.

empathy: The recognition of another's feelings and the **Truth** behind them. Goes beyond sympathy and compassion, which have us vicariously experiencing another's feelings without the related **Truth.**

fear: One of the four **core emotions**; a lack of knowing.

frontier: The realm of possibility that exists when one embraces fear as his guide, then steps beyond convention and familiarity.

Gifting Way: The state of abundance and personal fulfillment that comes from living the natural law that **giving is receiving.**

Giveaway (Potlatch): A ceremonial event during which those who have accumulated surplus distribute it to those more in need.

giving is receiving: We first honor someone by giving an offering, then we may be gifted in return.

healing: To bring a fractured, repressed self into ever-present wholeness; results in uninhibited flow of energy, **authenticity**, and **ego** reduction.

healing touch: Using physical touch from another as a way to dissolve boundaries, reduce inflammation, and release the **tribal hormone**.

Heart-of-Hearts: The center of one's being and seat of personal **Balance** where feelings, intuition, ancestral memories, the senses, and mental input come together to give perspective and guidance.

Hoop of Life (Hoop of Relations, Web of Life): The community of Plant, Animal, Mineral and Sky beings who live together in **Balance**.

joy: One of the four **core emotions**; a state of bliss we naturally find ourselves in when we are fully aware and attuned to the moment.

limbic mind (limbic track/system): The seat of our subconscious emotional functioning and memory; our primary brain functioning; the source of our gut feelings, attractions, repulsions, and all of those urges that are hard to explain or resist.

longing: One of the four **core emotions**; the ever-present thirst for relationships and the glue that keeps us in them.

mental illness: An erroneous concept devised by modern culture that entails the labeling of a person's subjective experience of self and world as symptomatic of a disorder—as something that contradicts the "objective" truth of the way things are.

Native: A plant or animal living a natural life in their natural habitat; a person living a hunter-gatherer lifestyle.

(Native) Elder: An aged community or clan member who is highly regarded as a bearer of inter-generational clan knowledge, a keeper of traditions, and a source of guidance based on wisdom drawn from life experience and ancestral memories.

natural: Intrinsic to a species or system.

Old Way: The Traditional lifestyle and practices intrinsic to hunter-gatherers.

Path: The direction of one's life.

rational mind (neocortical track, neocortical system, primate brain): The part of the brain that is responsible for our conscious, studied approach to life—shoulds, shouldn'ts, planning, projecting, etc.

sadness: One of the four **core emotions**; the state of being unable to give.

teaching trail: A way of living that entails engaging in our life process, becoming sensitized to our feelings and needs, exploring possibilities, gaining knowledge, learning skills, and growing in relationship.

tribal hormone: Oxytocin released through **healing touch** by a member of the clan.

true self (essential self, core self): Our intrinsic, **authentic** personality that emanates from the **limbic mind.**

Truth: An expression from the **Heart-of-Hearts** that stands above reproach because it is valid only for the individual who speaks it.

Truthspeaking: Concise, straight-from-the-heart expression of personal reality. Engenders trust and strengthens relationship.

Index

Acknowledgments

As the reluctant author of a book on emotional healing, I needed all the help and encouragement I could get. Fortunately, it came in abundance, from those who initially urged me to take on the project to the team that came together to craft my meanderings into something useful.

With this book being a decade in the making, and with my memory being what it is, I am likely to miss a person or two who made noteworthy contributions. Please know that your omission is not intentional, and that I regard your input just as highly as that of those whose identities, by some twist of fate, were retained in my memory long enough to be recorded here on this page.

First, I wish to acknowledge the numerous elders from a variety of cultures whom I served and worked with over the span of my life. Their guidance and stories have provided the foundational philosophies upon which this book is based, as well as many of the insights and examples I used. In the same breath, I wish to recognize the Wolves in the pack I lived with when I was a young man. They taught me emotional honesty in a language I could understand.

Right from the beginning, Andrew Huff worked with me to organize text and research source material. Nan Casper transcribed a good share of the text from my voice recordings. Snow Wolf Publishing's managing editor Alexandra Steussy-Williams coordinated every phase of the project, and she partnered with Snow Wolf editor Samantha Sprole to give the text its first edit. Brett Winters then created the index and glossary, along with formalizing the citations. Next came Rebecca deVogel's final edit, followed by input from what in publishing circles is known as the beta reader team, who gave the finished manuscript its all-important critical first read. They were Clinton Brown, Jordan Deffenbaugh, Nathan Hitchcock, Zoë Martinini, and Jason Moser. Then came the last step: the alchemistic skills of book designer Jim Arneson of JAAD Book Design, illustrator Peggy Grinvalsky, and e-book creator Tony Roberts of The Roberts Group Editorial and Design. To each and all of these talented and caring people, I extend my deepest gratitude.

Throughout the entire creation process, one person was continually there for me, giving support and guidance whenever needed. My dear beloved, Lucy Seibel, makes it hard for me to imagine how I could give as much as I receive from her.

About the Author

From an abusive childhood to dancing with suicide, living with Wolves, work on doctorates in Nature-based healing and adult recovery from childhood trauma, and decades of working with Native Elders, therapists, and holistic healthcare practitioners, Tamarack Song has come to know the intimacies of emotional healing.

Tamarack now teaches wilderness skills and serves as an instructor for outdoor guides, nature-based healers, and trauma therapists. He has written thirty books on Nature, healing, parenting, and cultural change-related topics, he serves as a consultant for environmental restoration projects and intentional communities, and he presents workshops on Zen, primal parenting, intimate relationships, Truth-speaking, emotional healing, shamanic soul retrieval, Nature aware-ness, archetypes, and founding and managing nonprofits.

The founder of natural food co-ops, alternative businesses, envi-ronmental groups, Brother Wolf Foundation, Teaching Drum Out-door School, Snow Wolf Publishing, and Healing Nature Center, he lives in a teaching-writing community nestled in Wisconsin's Nicolet National Forest. He can be reached at tamarack@healingnaturecen-ter.org.

To learn more about Tamarack Song's work, please visit these sites.

Brother Wolf Foundation

Since 1972, a voice for:
Renewing *the age-old human-Wolf relationship, and*
Creating *safe space for Wolves to run free.*
www.brotherwolffoundation.org

Healing Nature Trail & Center

Where Towering Pine and Whispering Breeze
Revitalize *body, mind, and spirit*
Release *pain, stress, and sorrow*
Renew *relationship with all of life.*
www.healingnaturecenter.org

Teaching Drum Outdoor School

Where wilderness is the classroom,
Ancient Voices are the teachers,
knowing self and balance is the quest.
www.teachingdrum.org

Snow Wolf Publishing

Crafter of quality books for
Remembering *what it is to be human,*
Restoring *our primal health, and*
Rediscovering *the world of Nature.*
www.snowwolfpublishing.org

Made in the USA
Monee, IL
17 July 2023

38840951R00150